FREDERICK

LOCAL AND NATIONAL CROSSROADS

Participants in a patriotic ceremony held during the 1920s gathered at the Francis Scott Key monument erected in his memory at Mount Olivet Cemetery. Frederick Mayor Lloyd C. Culler stands at the far left. (Courtesy of the Historical Society of Frederick County.)

Front Cover: *The Frederick High School Band poses for a photo c. 1924 with band leader S. Fenton Harris. (Courtesy of the Historical Society of Frederick County.)*

THE MAKING OF AMERICA

FREDERICK
LOCAL AND NATIONAL CROSSROADS

CHRIS HEIDENRICH

ARCADIA

Published by Arcadia Publishing,
an imprint of Tempus Publishing, Inc.
Charleston SC, Chicago, Portsmouth NH, San Francisco

Printed in Great Britain.

Library of Congress Catalog Card Number: 2003111114

For all general information contact Arcadia Publishing at:
Telephone 843-853-2070
Fax 843-853-0044
E-Mail sales@arcadiapublishing.com
For customer service and orders:
Toll-Free 1-888-313-2665

Visit us on the Internet at http://www.arcadiapublishing.com

CONTENTS

ACKNOWLEDGMENTS

This book could not have been completed without the assistance of several institutions and people. The photo, postcard, and map collections of the Historical Society of Frederick County provided most of the images used in this book. The Maryland Room of the C. Burr Artz Public Library also provided images. Both institutions' books, newspapers, vertical files, and other textual resources also provided much of the information that forms the basis for this book.

Many thanks to the Historical Society for its support of and assistance with this project. Thanks especially to Marie Washburn, the Historical Society librarian, who generously provided assistance with the organization's photos and other archival resources. Thanks also to Executive Director Mark Hudson and Resource Development Coordinator Duane K. Doxzen for their enthusiasm.

Employees of the Maryland Room at C. Burr Artz Public Library provided much advice and support. Thanks to Waneta Gagne, Maryland Room librarian and archivist, for her assistance with the photo and history collections and for her many helpful suggestions. Thanks also to Maryland Room Manager Mary Mannix for her early advice and encouragement, and continuing assistance.

Several other staff members and volunteers at the Historical Society and the library provided cheerful and helpful assistance.

Materials held by the Maryland State Archives and the Frederick County Chamber of Commerce also were consulted for this book. Mark Zeigler loaned an image of the 1917 Frederick Hustlers baseball team.

Several accomplished historians graciously volunteered their time to proofread and edit the manuscript, and offer suggestions. Kathryn M. Kuranda, Kirsten Peeler, and Janet Davis provided helpful editing and suggestions, and helped ensure that the manuscript accurately told the story of Frederick. Katherine Grandine read the introduction, provided several helpful suggestions for the rest of the book, and was a good sounding board. Frank Lipo, a friend and former colleague, read portions of the manuscript and offered helpful suggestions from the outside perspective of a historian based in the Midwest. However, any errors in any part of this book are entirely mine.

Thanks to Kirsten Peeler and J.B. Pelletier for the use of their laptop computers. I am indebted to Jim Kempert and Sarah Williams of Arcadia Publishing for their extensive advice and editorial support. Thanks to R. Christopher Goodwin, Ph.D., for his support.

Finally, I want to thank my friends and family, particularly my parents, for their unceasing support and encouragement.

INTRODUCTION

Maryland was a British colony in 1744. Prince George's County encompassed all of western Maryland: an area extending northeast of present-day Washington, D.C. to the current state's western border. In that year, lawyer, politician, and land speculator Daniel Dulany bought a 7,000-acre estate located west of the Monocacy River. Soon he subdivided a section along Carroll Creek, a tributary of the river. Dulany sought to attract settlers to lease lots and establish roots in his new community.

Native people had long valued the area for its rich land, rivers, and wildlife. Maryland's Proprietor, Charles Calvert, had opened western Maryland for settlement 12 years earlier in 1732, and several other speculators were granted large tracts in the area. Dulany's speculation proved correct, and Frederick Town was born.

Frederick Town, the colonial name for the present-day city of Frederick, became a crossroads linking Atlantic Coast settlements to the western frontier, and linking New England and the mid-Atlantic with settlements in the Shenandoah Valley of Virginia and southern colonies.

Many came to Frederick Town to live and to build a community. Settlers migrated from the east and the north seeking undeveloped land and opportunity. Immigrants from other countries arrived in search of a better life. The first settlers were predominantly English and German, but gradually the town's population represented many cultures, religions, and walks of life. Frederick Town's early residents built businesses, schools, churches, organizations, and government. Like many places in the United States, the history of Frederick is the story of growth from a frontier outpost to a small town to a city whose fortunes are linked to the region, the country, and the world. Frederick also occupies a unique place in U.S. history. Because Frederick is strategically located in the Mid-Atlantic region close to the nation's capital, the city has provided a stage and the actors for nationally significant events.

The roots of human habitation in the Frederick area stretch back thousands of years. Evidence of Indian settlement dates from as early as 10,000 B.C. European explorers, traders, and missionaries reached the Potomac River and its northern tributary through Frederick County, the Monocacy River, in the 1600s and early 1700s. In 1727, Benjamin Tasker, president of the governor's council of Maryland, received title to Tasker's Chance. Dulany bought Tasker's Chance 17 years later and laid out lots. By 1748, Frederick County was divided from Prince George's County, and Frederick Town became the county seat.

Generally, the Frederick Town area attracted English settlers from the east who sought new land on which to grow tobacco. Germans from Pennsylvania traveling south toward the less populated Shenandoah Valley of Virginia were attracted by the rich farmland they saw in Frederick County.

In the Revolutionary period, Frederick Town shared the growing frustration with British rule. In 1765, the Frederick County court repudiated the British Stamp Act, the first official act of rebellion in the colonies. During the Revolutionary War, no fighting occurred near Frederick Town, but barracks on South Market Street housed Hessian and English prisoners. Resident Thomas Johnson became Maryland's first governor in 1777, and in 1781, resident John Hanson was elected president of the Congress of the United States as Assembled, before the current federal government was created.

As the nineteenth century dawned, Frederick Town was maintained by an agricultural economy, but the growing town was developing businesses and industries, and remained an actor in the new nation. In 1806, Congress authorized construction of the first national highway, the National Road. The road passed through Frederick when the Baltimore to Frederick turnpike was incorporated into it. Frederick was the alternate seat of the federal government during the War of 1812. A branch of the Baltimore and Ohio Railroad arrived in 1831.

People from many backgrounds lived here, including Germans, English, Irish, and French. African Americans lived here since Frederick's beginnings, some in freedom, but many in slavery. Organized religions included Lutheran, Evangelical Reformed, Episcopal, Baptist, Catholic, Jewish, Methodist, and Presbyterian.

As the country teetered at the brink of a civil war, few Frederick residents supported the abolitionist cause, but the population was fiercely divided between supporters of southern secession and advocates of preserving the Union. Tensions were high because Maryland was a slave state and the secessionist states lay just over the southern border. The U.S. Supreme Court, led by Chief Justice Roger Brooke Taney, a former Frederick resident, issued its Dred Scott Decision declaring that slaves were not citizens and that Congress had no authority to restrict slavery in the territories, inflaming the country's divisions. John Brown heightened the divisions in 1859 when he raided the government arsenal in Harper's Ferry, Virginia, just south of Frederick County.

The Civil War disrupted the lives of residents. Frederick became the headquarters of the command of the Army of the Potomac in fall 1861. During the September 1862 Battle of Antietam, in Washington County west of Frederick, wounded soldiers from both sides were transported to Frederick. Churches, schools, homes, and the barracks were transformed into hospitals. The makeshift hospitals were pressed into service again to treat the sick and wounded in 1863 during the Battle of Gettysburg and in 1864 during the Battle of the Monocacy. Confederate troops invaded Frederick a second time in 1864, and city officials scrambled to pay a $200,000 ransom to prevent the Confederates from destroying the city.

After the war, Frederick slowly recovered. The Maryland School for the Deaf opened at the former Revolutionary War barracks in 1867. Free, but segregated, African Americans built strong communities around churches, schools, and businesses. Industry and technology helped lift the town. Manufacturers arrived in the 1880s and 1890s. Trolley and train lines were installed. In 1893, the Frederick Female Seminary became the Woman's College of Frederick, later renamed Hood College. Grand homes were built.

Frederick rode the national highs and lows of the first half of the twentieth century. World War I sent soldiers to battle in 1917, and influenza struck in 1918. Technology made possible improved city infrastructure and increased residents' mobility and entertainment options. The popularization of the automobile brought visitors downtown on the newly designated U.S. Route 40. The Tivoli movie palace opened. However, the city struggled to attract sustainable industry. The Depression struck in 1929, closing banks and businesses. In World War II, Frederick residents bought war bonds, conducted paper drives, and used ration coupons. The army developed a camp at an airfield on Frederick's northwestern outskirts. Camp Detrick opened in 1943.

In the 1950s, road construction, retail development, and the federal expansion of the army installation brought money, residents, and growth. The postwar boom was characterized by positive and negative changes. In 1956, Camp Detrick was made permanent and renamed Fort Detrick. Frederick Community College opened in 1957. African-American students began attending Frederick's public elementary and high schools in 1958. Construction began on Interstates 70 and 270, which link Frederick with Baltimore and Washington, D.C. and shortened travel times. The Golden Mile retail corridor opened on Route 40 west of downtown, increasing the city's retail base but sapping downtown retail dollars.

Since the 1970s, Frederick has experienced a downtown revival and continued growth but in some respects maintains the feel of a relatively small town in a rural county. Interstates 270 and 70 were expanded and Route 15 was built, improving mobility. Train service between Frederick and Washington, D.C. was re-established in 2001. Both attracted more commuters to Frederick. Cultural outlets opened, such as the Weinberg Center for the Arts, located in the former Tivoli Theater. The Carroll Creek flood control project led to the creation of an attractive downtown linear park along the creek, and is contributing to downtown development by paving the way for reuse of land bordering the creek. Agriculture still plays a role in the local economy, but not as much as in the past.

Frederick: Local and National Crossroads is intended to provide an overview of Frederick history, to whet the reader's appetite. Enjoy this story of Frederick presented in words and images. Then walk the city streets or follow the old railroad tracks. Notice the architectural details in Frederick's historic buildings, and absorb views seen by people standing in the same spot many years earlier. Go to the Historical Society of Frederick County and the Maryland Room of the C. Burr Artz Library and read more about Frederick, especially in the sources listed in the bibliography of this volume. Dig into the multiple layers of Frederick's rich history.

Chapter One

NATIVE AMERICANS AND EUROPEAN SETTLERS (TO 1760)

The majority of native people had already migrated from the area when Frederick officially was established in 1745. Native Americans had used the Frederick area as a crossroads for thousands of years before European settlement. Several tribes lived, camped, and hunted here. They fished in the Monocacy River and its tributaries, settled on the riverbanks, hunted the abundant wildlife, cultivated the rich farmland, and established trails to link settlements and resources.

Archeologists have found evidence of Indian settlement in the Frederick area dating as far back as 10,000 B.C. This date marks the beginning of human habitation in the area after the glaciers receded. This time period began what archeologists call the Paleo-Indian Period, one of three major periods used to classify human habitation in North America before the arrival of Europeans. People of the Paleo-Indian Period were hunters who probably migrated across the Bering Straits when sea levels were lower. One of their distinctive tools was the fluted spear point. During the next period, the Archaic Period, between 8,000 B.C. and 1,000 B.C., people pursued a wider range of plants and animals. They were less mobile and less selective about the type of stone used to make their tools. This might have been because hunting was less important, or because fewer varieties of stone were available since they traveled less and the population was growing. In Frederick County, the mineral rhyolite began to be quarried from the mountains for refinement into spear points. Rhyolite only occurs naturally in the Frederick County area, but rhyolite pieces have been found throughout Maryland, indicating that people came to Frederick County from all over Maryland to quarry it. Meanwhile, pottery made of crushed oyster shells has been found in this area, indicating that local people traded with coastal residents.

The bow and arrow was not used on the East Coast until the third period, the Woodland Period, which spanned 1,000 B.C. to 1600 A.D. The Woodland-Period Indians also used clay to make pottery for eating utensils, and cultivated the land. They grew corn, tobacco, beans, peas, squash, and sunflowers. They continued to hunt, but lived in permanent villages. A tradition of myths and legends is believed to have begun during this period. One story is associated with Yellow Springs, located about 3 miles northwest of Frederick. The area was called Montonqua, meaning "Medicine Waters," because people believed the springs here were fed by the Great Spirit. Tribes preparing for battle came here to drink the water for strength and courage. Sick people were brought here to be bathed in the water and smeared with orange pigment from the stream bed. The pigment was sulphur, which led to the area being named Yellow Springs. The arrival of European settlers marked the end of the Woodland Period.

Indians settled along the Monocacy River, which flows north and south through present-day northeastern Frederick. The river provided both a transportation route and a food supply. Archeologists have identified hundreds of sites along the Monocacy. One of the most important of these sites is located at the Rosenstock farm, in northeastern Frederick. The site was a large circular village that was occupied during the fifteenth century. Large trash-filled pits and pottery from the site indicate that the residents' diet was diverse. Evidence of structures indicated that they were circular, about 15 feet in diameter, with a square entryway that gave the buildings the shape of an igloo or a keyhole. Archeologists theorize that these structures served a ceremonial purpose, such as a sweatlodge. The structures and the ceramics were similar to materials to the north, suggesting a cultural connection to areas in New York or northern Pennsylvania.

The Monocacy River's tributaries also supported prehistoric settlements. In 1959, rhyolite spear points, bowl fragments, and other artifacts were found on Schifferstadt farm, located on Carroll Creek at Second Street and Rosemont Avenue. In 1995, archeologist Hettie Ballweber found the base of a hearth, spear points, and more rhyolite. This evidence suggested that the site was a base camp and that rhyolite was transported via the creek from the mountains to the site, where it was processed into tools. The site was ideal for occupation because it sat on an elevated terrace overlooking the creek, Ballweber said in the 1999 documentary *Monocacy: The Pre-History of Frederick County*.

Other sites of Indian habitation in the Frederick vicinity have been found along Linganore Creek, an eastern tributary of the Monocacy, and several along Tuscarora Creek, a western tributary just north of Frederick. In 1946, the Baltimore *Sun* reported on a Frederick electrician's extensive collection of arrowheads gathered in the Worman's Mill area on Frederick's northern boundary. Pottery, charred animal bones, and burial sites have been identified at Biggs Ford, between Frederick and Walkersville. Occupied between 1000 and 1600 A.D., this site is one of the largest prehistoric villages in Maryland. Twelve burials were found at this site. Some bodies were folded, indicating that they were buried in winter when the ground was hard and large holes were difficult to dig. Bodies laid out fully were buried in warmer weather. Bows and arrows and smoking pipes were buried with some bodies. With such finds, it is easy to relate to these human ancestors from thousands of years ago, according to Bill Davis, an archeology expert who spoke in the Monocacy documentary:

> It's easy for us to look at these human burials and to imagine in our minds all the human emotions that would have gone along with that, the profound sorrow and sense of loss that's associated with the loss of a child as the mother places the baby in the grave and puts a small clay pot beside it. Or the reverence and deep respect these folks had for this hunter and warrior as they placed him in the grave and put with him his bow and arrow and other personal possessions.

Native Americans and European Settlers

Rock shelters, which were temporary shelters Indians used while traveling during hunting or rock quarrying expeditions, also are located in Frederick County. Boyers Mill Rock Shelter is the largest known rock shelter in the county and is located a few miles east of Frederick near Lake Linganore. This rock shelter was used intermittently over a 5,000-year period.

Archeologists prefer to classify Native American habitation in terms of cultural periods rather than tribes, because archeological excavations yield more evidence of the ways people lived and functioned, rather than their tribal histories. Nevertheless, some information is available on the various tribes or groups of Native Americans who lived in the Frederick area in the years just before the arrival of Europeans. The Delawares, Shawnees, Tuscaroras, Monocans, and Senecas hunted and fought in Frederick County during the Woodland Period. During the 1500s, the Susquehannocks of Pennsylvania traveled south to raid hunting areas in Frederick County. At this time, native people might have left the area for southern Maryland when resources were depleted. The Susquehannocks claimed Maryland from the Chesapeake Bay to the western border, and ceded it to the English in 1652. However, organized European settlement did not occur for approximately 70 more years, and Indians returned to Frederick County in 1699, when the Piscataways moved to southern Frederick County to flee white encroachment on their lands in Charles and Prince George's Counties.

During the early 1700s, groups associated with the Iroquois claimed all of western Maryland and fought for control against the Susquehannocks and the Nanticokes. Gradually, defeated smaller tribes moved away. The Susquehannocks fled south after being decimated by smallpox, and the Iroquois groups moved closer to the centers of their nations, vacating Frederick County by about 1712. Many of the Piscataways also had left, migrating to Pennsylvania. In 1744, chiefs of the Six Nations signed a treaty with the Maryland colony relinquishing their rights to land in Maryland.

Thus ended thousands of years of Native American occupation. Their influence is evident in Indian names such as Chesapeake and Monocacy. Clues to their presence are found throughout Frederick County, according to archeologist Hettie Ballweber:

> In Frederick County today, if a person was to go into their back yard and dig a hole to plant a tree or to plant something in their vegetable garden and they find an arrowhead or a spear point, they think that is quite a find. But in the county, that's not an uncommon occurrence, because Frederick County was intensely occupied throughout the prehistoric period by groups. That's because . . . as beautiful as Frederick County is today, and as attractive as it is for people to live here today, it was just as attractive for people in the prehistoric time to live here. It had all the resources people needed. Almost everywhere along the streams and rivers today you can find evidence of prehistoric occupation.

Individuals and small groups of European explorers began arriving before Indian habitation ended. For instance, Henry Fleet explored the upper Potomac in 1624, ten years before the first permanent European settlers arrived in Maryland, and wrote a description of an area that might have been today's southern Frederick County. Around 1640, missionaries who accompanied Maryland's first white settlers established an outpost along the Monocacy River just east of present-day Frederick. Also in the 1600s, a man named Cartier or Chartier traded with Indians at the junction of the Potomac and the Monocacy, in southern Frederick County. He closed his post when the Indians left the area. As an indication of European settlement in Maryland, western Maryland was given its own government in 1699, when Prince George's County was established.

In the early 1700s, the Swiss explorer Franz-Louis Michel traveled along the Monocacy east of present-day Frederick. Michel came to the area to identify potential Swiss settlement sites. He and a Maryland settler named Clark explored southern Frederick County and made their way north along the Monocacy. They crossed Carroll Creek near its mouth, in the vicinity of northeastern Frederick. Michel drew a map of the area and returned to Switzerland. Soon afterward, Swiss explorer Christoph von Graffenreid mapped southern Frederick County, including the Potomac and Monocacy Rivers, Sugarloaf Mountain, and Point of Rocks.

Meanwhile, squatters probably began occupying land in the Frederick vicinity and in the larger present-day Frederick County. These squatters did not officially own the land, so their names are unrecorded. The first official land transaction in present-day Frederick County occurred in 1718, when Arthur Nelson bought land near Point of Rocks. Settlement began to increase gradually. John Van Meter acquired approximately 300 acres along Reel's Mill Road southeast of present-day Frederick in 1724. The next year he acquired more land, expanding his holdings along Carroll Creek east from South Market and South Street to the fairgrounds. He and his family lived on the latter parcel until 1735 and built four houses. The Prince George's County Court appointed him constable for several terms between 1729 and 1734. Between 1724 and 1743, Thomas Albin lived on land along the Monocacy now occupied by Frederick Municipal Airport.

Because of its income potential, increasing western settlement caught the attention of "men of means" in Annapolis and on the Eastern Shore. Grace L. Tracey and John P. Dern, in their 1987 study, *Pioneers of Old Monocacy: The Early Settlement of Frederick County, Maryland 1721–1743*, succinctly explained what happened next:

> Income, they discovered, could be made from rentals and sales of the land farther to the west. But if there was to be wealth in the land, they had best stake their claims by nailing down title to that land. This was naturally also of great benefit to Lord Baltimore, for his own recompense lay largely in the recurring annual quitrents payable to him once title to the land had passed to individuals. So began an era when speculators or land investors surveyed rather large tracts of land, not with the intention of living on that land, but with the hope of sizeable subsequent profit from others settling there.

The first property surveyed in present-day Frederick County was the 2,800-acre "Hope" tract in southeastern Frederick County, in 1721. The 16th survey in the county is the one most relevant to Frederick city history. Benjamin Tasker, a wealthy former Annapolis mayor and a future Commissary General and President of the Maryland Council, had a 7,000-acre parcel along Carroll Creek surveyed in 1725. "Tasker's Chance" was located immediately west of the Monocacy River. It stretched approximately 4 miles north of the mouth of Carroll Creek and 2 to 4 miles west of the Monocacy. Frederick Town was laid out on the south end 20 years later, in 1745.

Surveys were conducted as part of the Maryland colony's procedure for obtaining land. The Maryland land office conducted a survey after an interested party made a purchase payment and applied for a warrant requesting a survey of a specified number of acres of unoccupied land. The land office issued the warrant, which instructed the Maryland surveyor general to appoint a deputy for the appropriate county. The deputy viewed the parcel and issued a certificate of survey that summarized the land's location, size, shape, and physical features, and adjacent properties. A diagram of the property also was provided. The land office checked to make sure the new parcel did not encroach on existing land grants, recorded the information, and issued a patent that granted title, subject to an annual "quitrent," a form of property tax paid to the Proprietor. Tasker's patent was issued in 1727. Settlers on Tasker's land negotiated deeds within the patent directly with Tasker.

The colony's land office had been surveying parcels such as Tasker's Chance for 11 years, but Lord Baltimore did not officially open western lands for settlement until 1732. This proclamation and two other events combined to help bring English settlers from eastern Maryland and German farmers from Pennsylvania. After nearly 100 years of settlement, eastern Maryland was becoming crowded and tobacco cultivation had worn out the land. Germans were moving south from Pennsylvania because land was becoming similarly scarce in that colony and because Virginia Governor Dinwiddie had issued an invitation to settle in western Virginia. The major route south from Pennsylvania to Virginia followed the Monocacy River through Frederick County. Many Germans were enticed to settle in western Maryland instead of Virginia because they liked Lord Baltimore's settlement terms and Frederick County's rich farmland.

Contrary to the popular belief that Frederick was first settled by Germans, English settlers predominated in the area with only a few German settlers present, according to a 1733 list of the taxable residents of the area. C.E. Schildknecht, who reviewed this tax list for Volume One of his book *Monocacy and Catoctin: Some Early Settlers of Frederick and Carroll Counties, MD and Adams County PA and Descendants 1725–1985*, found that this tax list contained names of many English who were former residents of southern Maryland. Schildknecht asserted that a few German families were present but could not obtain deeds because they were poor and did not speak English. Schildknecht believed that surviving naturalization and church records might have given the impression that Germans made up the majority of European settlers to the area. German and Swiss immigrants arriving in Philadelphia from 1728 to the Revolution were carefully documented and immediately required to take the oath of allegiance to England, while English immigrants to America were not. Also, western Maryland churches that served Germans, such as German Reformed, Lutheran, and Moravian, preserved more complete records than did the Catholic, Episcopal, and Presbyterian churches with the English speaking congregations.

The 1733 tax record also provides the first evidence of slaves in the Frederick vicinity. Two were listed. They might not have been the first blacks in the area. Possibly as early as the 1720s, freed and runaway slaves from other areas fled to the mountains west of present-day Frederick and lived with Indians.

Germans began entering Frederick County from Pennsylvania in greater numbers in the 1730s. The story behind German settlement in Frederick and the surrounding Frederick County begins 50 years earlier. In the late 1600s, William Penn, the Proprietor of Pennsylvania, circulated fliers in Germany to seek settlers for his colony, and visited Germany himself in 1681 to make a personal pitch for the settlement. His offer was tempting to Germans weary of the destructive Thirty Years' War and French raids under Louis XIV, which ruined farmland and threw many into poverty. Other difficulties included heavy taxation, a lack of open land, and the brutal winter of 1708. Meanwhile, the British government changed its Naturalization Act in 1709, making it easier for foreign Protestants to settle on British land. Germans emigrating to Pennsylvania first entered through Philadelphia. Many eventually made their way west to the Pennsylvania counties of Adams and Lancaster, located north of Maryland's Frederick County.

When the Pennsylvania Germans started moving south with regularity in the 1730s, they used routes formerly used by Native Americans and, later, traders. The route from Pennsylvania branched into two roads, which the historians Tracey and Dern described as the German Monocacy Road (named for the identity of most of its users) and the Manor Monocacy Road. "Monocacy" indicated both roads directed travelers west toward the Monocacy River and wound along the river. Both roads skirted Frederick as they traveled south into Virginia. The routes began as one road originating in Conestoga, a German area of Pennsylvania located north and east of Lancaster. The road traveled south through Adams and York Counties and crossed the Monocacy in northern Frederick County. West of the river, near present-day Thurmont, the road divided into two branches.

The German Monocacy Road traveled west through Graceham, and then, similar to today's Route 15, turned south through Jimtown Crossroads and Lewistown. The route crossed the intersection of present-day Butterfly Lane and Mount Phillip Road, in southwestern Frederick. The road then traveled west through present-day Middletown and Washington County, and across the Potomac River into Virginia. In 1745, an eastern connection was built between this road and the Monocacy. As evidence of the number of Germans who used the road, 33 of the 36 land surveys conducted between May 10, 1738 and December 10, 1743 along the road between Jimtown Crossroads and Butterfly Lane were for German settlers. The Swiss explorer Michel might have traveled part of this route when he visited the area in 1707.

The other branch, the Manor Monocacy Road, turned south near present-day Thurmont and recrossed the river, continuing south on the river's east side to Hughes Ford, where it crossed the river again. This crossing was located at the south end of the plantation of one of the area's early settlers, Thomas Albin, and east of present-day

Frederick Municipal Airport. The river crossing also was the same ford used by Michel in 1707. From the river, the road traveled south along the west side of the Monocacy to the river's mouth in southern Frederick County. The German Monocacy Road appears to have had greater traffic than the Manor Monocacy Road. Landowners of large parcels commissioned most of the surveys along the road on the east side of the river.

As more settlers arrived, another branch of the Monocacy Manor Road was built in 1749 along much of present-day Route 194. The branch extended south from Keysville, at a point where the German Monocacy and Monocacy Manor roads were still one. The branch traveled through Woodsboro and Walkersville and met the original Monocacy Manor Road just east of the river and present-day northeastern Frederick.

After 1736, many Germans traveled these roads to migrate south into Frederick County. Most of the settlers on Tasker's Chance were German, and most belonged to the German Reformed Church. One settler was Joseph Brunner, a widower enticed to move south from Pennsylvania with his children upon hearing of Lord Baltimore's land deal. As early as 1736, Brunner and his family might have occupied land in present-day Frederick at the corner of Second Street and Rosemont Avenue. Daniel Dulany granted Brunner a deed for 303 acres at that location, and Brunner or a family member built the oldest house surviving in present-day Frederick, Schifferstadt, in 1756. The stone house was named for Brunner's birthplace, Kleinschifferstadt, Germany, and is preserved as an outstanding example of German colonial architecture.

Six other German settlers had tried to buy Tasker's Chance from Benjamin Tasker in 1737. The syndicate could not raise the funds, and land speculator Daniel Dulany acquired the tract. Dulany was a lawyer and member of the Maryland Assembly who arrived in Maryland from Ireland in 1703 as an indentured servant. He started investing in land in this area in the 1720s. Dulany received title to Tasker's Chance in 1744. His objective was to develop a town that could trade with England.

Dulany's purchase paved the way for the establishment of the town of Frederick. Its creation would not have been possible just three years earlier. Johann Jost Schmidt, one of the six German settlers who had tried earlier to buy Tasker's Chance, occupied 500 acres that later included the site of Frederick Town. However, by the time Dulany purchased Tasker's Chance, Schmidt appeared to have left the area. As a condition of the sale of Tasker's Chance, Dulany was required to confer land titles to current occupants; no title was issued to Schmidt. Dulany retained title to the land formerly occupied by Schmidt.

The year 1745 is commonly recognized for the establishment of Frederick, marking the year that Dulany is believed to have laid out the town. Some claim Dulany surveyed the town in September 1745, but others say that no conclusive evidence pinpoints the exact date when the lots were laid out, because Dulany never filed an official, dated plan. One clue appears in a document written by a visiting Lutheran pastor named Gabriel Nasman on October 31, 1746. Nasman added a "Friederichs Tawn" dateline to the document, suggesting that the town existed at that time. Another clue lies in the dates Dulany set for lot owners to pay annual quitrents. Dulany granted the first deeds for town lots in 1748, but first received quitrents in 1746. It appears that some buyers paid for their lots over time and received title upon final payment. These installment purchasers paid quitrents immediately.

Dulany's plan for Frederick Town provided 144 rectangular lots in six rows of 24 lots each, along both sides of Carroll Creek. The lots measured 60 feet by 393 feet. Lot 1 was located on the northwest corner of All Saints and Carroll Streets, and this first row extended west to Record Street. The numbering of the rest of the rows alternated east and west, ending with Lot 144 on the west side of Carroll straddling Third and Fourth Streets. Occupants paid an upfront fee of £2 and then 1 shilling a year for the first 20 years, and 2 shillings the subsequent years. They owned the buildings constructed on the lots, but if they defaulted on the land rent, Dulany acquired the buildings. Lots were added north and south of the original lots, so that by 1764 the town comprised approximately 343 lots, bounded roughly by North Street (today's Seventh Street), south of South Street, East, Carroll, and Bentz Streets.

Dulany laid out the streets in straight lines, except for Patrick Street. He designed a bend on West Patrick Street, possibly to avoid marshy, less stable land. Dulany named the new settlement "Frederick Town," probably to honor Frederick Calvert, sixth and last Lord Baltimore.

The first house believed to have been built in the new town stood at the northeast corner of Middle Alley and East Patrick Street. It was built by John Thomas Schley, who received the deed to a lot in 1746. In 1712, Schley was born in Morzheim, Germany (today a Sister City of Frederick), and later moved to his wife's hometown of Appenhofen, where he is believed to have recruited 100 settlers to move with him to Frederick. Schley was active in his new community. He was a schoolteacher, a lay leader in the Reformed Church, and a tavern owner. The house was torn down in approximately 1856.

One of the priorities for the new town was to establish churches. Dulany donated Lot 64, the second lot west of Market Street between Patrick and Church Streets, to the Evangelical Reformed Church in 1746. In 1747, the denomination built a log church and a school, the first in Frederick Town, with Schley serving as schoolmaster. The denomination replaced its church in 1764 and constructed a tall wooden steeple with a clock on the site in 1807. In 1880 the church was torn down, rebuilt, and rededicated as Trinity Chapel in 1882 for use as a church school. A church was constructed on its present location on the north side of West Church Street in 1848.

German Lutherans had begun settling in the Frederick vicinity in the 1730s, and by 1746 built a church on the north side of East Church Street on one of the initial 144 lots in Frederick Town. In 1753 the congregation began construction of a larger church on the same site, but work was interrupted by the French and Indian War, and the church was not completed until 1762. The present church, with its twin spires, was completed on the same site in 1855.

The other major church established in Frederick Town was the "establishment" denomination of the colony, the Church of England. Present-day Frederick County was included in the vast Prince George's Parish, which encompassed Prince George's County. Two hundred western Maryland residents petitioned in 1742 to establish their own parish, so that they could meet their religious needs closer to home. All Saints Parish was created and ministered to present-day Montgomery County, part of Carroll County, Frederick County, and the rest of western Maryland. In 1747, the Maryland Assembly authorized a tax on all inhabitants of the parish to raise £300 to buy 3 acres in Frederick Town and build a church on it. The Assembly authorized another tax levy to complete the church in 1750. This church was located on the north side of East All Saints Street. The church moved to North Court Street in 1814. The Court Street church became the parish house when the present church was constructed on West Church Street in 1856.

The Church of England truly was the "establishment." A 1723 law establishing a free school in each county of Maryland required that schoolmasters belong to the Church of England. Every taxable resident, regardless of their religious denomination, was taxed to build and maintain Church of England churches. Sampson Lazarus, a merchant who lived on East Patrick Street, was responsible for keeping all streets that led to All Saints Church in passable condition. But the church was no longer the establishment when the Revolution occurred; British Loyalists in Frederick had their property confiscated.

Members of other religious groups were represented in early Frederick, including Jews and Roman Catholics. Paul and Rita Gordon, in their 1971 book *The Jews Beneath the Clustered Spires,* documented that the first Jewish resident in Frederick Town was Henry Lazarus in 1742. Henry Lazarus & Co. filed a lawsuit in 1752 that referred to a promissory note drawn up ten years earlier, suggesting that Lazarus was established in Frederick Town as early as 1742. Lazarus signed his 1778 will in Hebrew. Newspapers and legal documents sometimes referred to Jews by their religion; people belonging to other faiths were not identified by religion. Other early Jews in Frederick County included Henry Roth, who bought the 323-acre "Olio" property from Daniel Dulany in 1746, and Benjamin Levy, who ran a business in Frederick from 1751 to 1763. Jews met for worship, but a rabbi did not arrive in the community until the late 1850s, and the first synagogue was not built until 1923.

Roman Catholics also have an extensive history in Frederick. The first Roman Catholics arrived in Frederick Town in the 1750s as part of a larger western migration of Catholics west from the seat of government in Annapolis. These settlers sought a sparsely settled area to escape persecution by the leaders of the Maryland Province, who were associated with the Church of England. Maryland's first English settlers, who arrived in 1634, were Catholic, but their fortunes turned when Protestants overthrew England's Catholic leaders in 1688. After that time, Maryland's laws were not friendly to Catholics. In 1718, for instance, the Maryland Assembly disenfranchised Catholics. The first Catholic institution in Frederick Town was a school for boys established in 1756 on Market Street, the beginnings of St. John's Literary Institute. Since Catholics were not allowed to build their own churches, Father John Williams, an English Jesuit, built the first church, St. John's, in 1763 on the northwest corner of Second Street and Chapel Alley as part of his private residence. Because of anti-Catholic laws, the building was owned not by the Catholic Church but by a private citizen, John Carey. He conveyed the lot to the Church in 1765. Work on the first church building, on the same site, was begun in 1800 and completed in 1812. The cornerstone was laid for the present church, across Second Street, in 1833 and it was consecrated in 1837. The church consisted mostly of English and Irish parishioners, with some German and black members as well.

Soon after Frederick Town was laid out, Dulany acted to ensure that the new settlement would function as a center of commerce. In 1746, merely a year after its founding, Dulany received a permit from Charles Calvert, Maryland's Proprietor, to operate a weekly market for buying and selling cattle and various provisions. The following year, in fall 1747, Dulany sponsored a fair that he hoped would become an annual event. He might have been attempting to bring together English and German settlers for an event in which a good time could be had by all. Apparently, the scheme worked. The first fair featured horseracing, a sport imported from England. The sport was new to the Germans but they quickly became fans.

Within a few years of Frederick Town's founding, the community claimed a population of craftsmen working in carpentry, blacksmithing, leathercraft, weaving, and tailoring. More than 50 craftsmen were documented in Frederick Town in its first 20 years. Other occupations represented in the town included painters, butchers, coopers, and merchants. Professionals included those involved in medicine, education, and law. These occupations were compiled in a list of early lot owners in Frederick Town published by Amy Lee Huffman Reed and Marie LaForge Burns in their 1985 book *In and Out of Frederick Town: Colonial Occupations*. Other occupations included miller, miner, breeches maker, brewer, shoemaker, saddler, brickmaker, hatter, glassmaker, gunsmith, and farmer. This variety in occupations helped sustain Frederick Town, since larger, established settlements were not nearby.

One of the first occupations in Frederick Town was that of innholder. Inns, or taverns, not only provided lodging to travelers but also provided a gathering place where locals could discuss current events and hear news from the traveling visitors. Operators were strictly regulated. They were required to obtain a license from the local court and renew it annually or face a hefty penalty of 40 shillings. Gambling on the Sabbath was forbidden, and prices for services were fixed by the court and revised annually. Kennedy Farrell operated the first tavern documented in Frederick Town, at the southwest corner of Market and Patrick Streets, possibly as early as 1747. It was in this two-story brick building that several Frederick County Circuit Court justices met in 1749 to write rules for electing the four Frederick County delegates to the Maryland Provincial Assembly. Subsequent owners operated the tavern until 1771, when the lot was subdivided and the corner sold to a blacksmith named Francis Mantz. Cleburn Simms received the first tavern license issued by the Frederick County court, in March 1749. When he died, his widow Mary Simms became the first woman licensed as an innholder in Frederick Town. Their tavern was located on the northeast corner of Patrick and Market.

Thomas Schley, the schoolteacher and religious leader who was one of the town's first settlers, also operated a tavern. He was fined in 1749 for operating without a license, indicating he might have been open before that year. The tavern probably was located in his home on the corner of Middle Alley and West Patrick Street. In June 1749, the court granted John Crampkin a license to operate a public house on East Second Street. His inventory indicates that he might have had more money than other tavern operators. He had six feather beds with English and Dutch blankets and white sheets rather than the brown ones typically used in the back country, four rugs, an oval table, pewter plates, and a black walnut table with matching chairs.

By 1748, western Maryland residents petitioned successfully to break away from Prince George's County and to form Frederick County. Petitions for a separate county had been filed with the Assembly every year for the previous nine years. This part of the colony still was sparsely settled; the new county encompassed an area much more vast than it does today. It was the largest county in Maryland. In addition to its present-day boundaries, Frederick County also included all of Montgomery, Washington, Allegany, and Garrett Counties, and parts of Carroll County. Frederick County's size was reduced in 1776 with the creation of Washington and Montgomery Counties. Frederick County assumed its current boundaries when Carroll County was formed from parts of Frederick and Baltimore Counties in 1836.

Frederick Town became the seat of the new county, probably because of Daniel Dulany's clout in Annapolis and the additional clout of Benjamin Tasker, the original owner of Tasker's Chance. The county courthouse was located here and all the county's business was conducted here. This distinction helped fuel Frederick Town's growth and economic development. Such government employees as clerks of the court and deputy clerks of the county moved to town. These employees were called scriveners, men who were skilled at copying legal documents. In their book, *In and Out of Frederick Town,* Reed and Burns called them "men of refinement and modest wealth," who had money to buy lots, build homes, and purchase goods. The county seat also brought in temporary visitors from all reaches of the county. These visitors required food and lodging while conducting their official business. They patronized Frederick Town businesses to satisfy these needs.

The county court met soon after the county's formation. Justices were appointed in December 1748. Millard Milburn Rice excerpted court records from the first years of the county court in his 1979 book, *This Was the Life.* Since the court was not only the governing body of the county, but also served as a civil and criminal court, this body oversaw all facets of colonial life. The record of court activities reveals many details about life at that time.

The court started meeting for routine business in March 1749 and met four times a year, in March, June, August, and November. Acting in a regulatory capacity, the justices made decisions related to the organization of the new county. For instance, they organized the county into 16 administrative units called hundreds, which were traditionally English divisions of land large enough to produce 100 soldiers from the inhabitants. A constable was appointed to oversee each hundred. Eighteen constables were designated in Frederick County because the Monocacy Hundred was divided into three parts, each with its own constable. Frederick Town was located in the middle part of Monocacy Hundred and served by constable Stephen Julian. Three people were appointed to lay out a road that led from Joseph Ogle's ford south to John Biggs' ford on the Monocacy River, and then south to Frederick Town. A petition was granted to lay out a road from Nelson's Ferry (near present-day Harper's Ferry) to Frederick Town. Today that road is Ballenger Creek Pike. George Gordon Jr. was appointed to buy a standard weight for the county. Rates were set for the sale of "liquors and other accommodations vendable in this County . . ." "Lodging in a bed per night" cost 6 pence, "syder per gallon" cost 2 shillings, "Maryland good strong beer per gallon sealed" cost 3 shillings, a stable and fodder for a horse cost 1 shilling per night, and corn and oats per bushel cost 4 shillings. The most expensive item on the rate list was peach brandy, which cost 13 shillings, four pence per gallon.

The court also protected the destitute and others who could not care for themselves. Orphan Simon Herden, estimated to be 8 or 9 years old, was bound to Charles Higginbothom, who promised to ensure that the child would be taught to read and write and would receive a suit when he reached 21. Martin Earnest received a tax exemption because of his financial hardship in caring for his four blind children.

Some of the court's activities shed light on period attitudes toward groups of people that would be unacceptable today. The grand jury met to consider charges against six women who gave birth while unmarried, known as "bastardy" (Rice stated that mostly women were brought before the court on this charge, and that he found only one or two cases involving male defendants). In a separate case, a female servant was tried in the June court on a charge of giving birth to a "mulatto" bastard child. She was found guilty of "general bastardy" and sentenced to receive five lashes on her bare body at the whipping post. She also was required to serve her master an additional nine months for the time and money he lost because of her pregnancy.

A court record from the June session reflected what Rice believed was English condescension toward Germans. Two elderly men with German surnames requested tax exemptions because they could no longer work. Instead of using standard spelling, the clerk copied their accented pronunciation, writing that the men had come to "bray the Court to be levy-free" instead of "pray," and that the men said they would be "danksfull in their lifetime for it," instead of "thankful."

One other important item of business that the justices attended to at their first session in March 1749 was the construction of a courthouse. Justices were meeting temporarily in the log German Reformed Church on Patrick Street, and the county's legal business needed a permanent location. They instructed the sheriff to advertise throughout the county for construction proposals that would be received on May 8. That year, the county purchased 3 acres from Daniel Dulany for the construction of the courthouse and a jail, lots 73 to 78, located east of Record Street between Church and Second Streets. Construction began immediately on the wood-frame, one-and-one-half story structure, located in the roadbed of present-day Council Street. The shell was completed on November 24, 1750. The French and Indian War delayed the completion of the interior until 1756. Interior construction required horses to haul materials, but draft animals were impressed for military service so that none were available for the courthouse project. A log jail also was part of the complex, along with a whipping post (an acceptable form of punishment at the time). This courthouse was in service for about 30 years, until a larger building was constructed in 1785.

Although social distinctions existed in Frederick Town, they were not as strict as they were in England. Mrs. Charlotte Brown, who came from England in 1755 to help nurse British troops wounded in the French and Indian War, discovered this and recorded her disapproval in her diary. She attended a ball in Frederick Town that "was composed of Romans, Hebrews, and Heretics who in this town flock together." The Romans were Catholics, the Hebrews were Jews, and the "Heretics" were German Protestants who were not members of the Church of England. She also noted with disapproval that the women wore no hoops or stays, and that each woman danced a jig at the end of the evening.

In 1755, the 10-year-old settlement had 200 houses and three churches. The French and Indian War turned the town into a crossroads for military planning and movement and for frightened settlers fleeing east. The war was part of the Seven Years War between England and France, in which each country vied for control of the western frontier. After colonizing New Orleans, France built a series of forts stretching from Louisiana to Canada. Construction of a fort at Pittsburgh, called Fort Duquesne, spurred the English to action in order to defend England's interests in North America. General Edward Braddock brought 1,400 British troops from England, and sought aid from the Shawnee and Delaware tribes. The French sought assistance from the Iroquois.

Frederick Town was the last large settlement before the wilderness, so Frederick Town was a staging area and meeting place for General Braddock and those assisting him from the colonies. A young George Washington was appointed Braddock's aide, and he was headquartered in a tavern on West All Saints Street, which was torn down in 1913 due to its dilapidated condition. Benjamin Franklin, the colonial postmaster general, provided advice and secured supplies. Some researchers claim that, contrary to popular belief, Franklin and Braddock probably were headquartered in a separate location from the small building in which Washington stayed, and that Washington and Franklin were in Frederick at different times.

Franklin and Washington agreed that General Braddock was arrogant, impatient, and condescending. Braddock was used to "civilized" wars of Europe and was ill-informed about the realities of fighting a war on the frontier, where few roads existed. Instead, Braddock expected to march with full baggage and other luxuries. He and his men required 200 wagons and 2,500 horses to carry baggage and weapons. These supplies were not readily available in Frederick or the vicinity, and Braddock waited with disgust while Franklin secured supplies in Pennsylvania on his own credit. A road to Duquesne did not exist in some areas, so one had to be built. Although he knew this, Braddock still insisted on traveling to the fort in a coach pulled by six horses.

Braddock also refused to heed advice that the Indians' guerrilla-style fighting would challenge the troops, who were accustomed to fighting an enemy in formal engagements. He informed Franklin that he believed he could take Fort Duquesne in three or four days and then march north to Canada. He also said of the Indians, "These savages may indeed be a formidable enemy to your raw American militia, but upon the

FREDERICK

King's regular and disciplined troops, sir, it is impossible they should make any impression." He refused Washington's pleas to allow Frederick County men wearing Indian dress to fight the Indians using the Indians' methods, because he believed the men to be undisciplined.

Predictably, with Braddock courting so much hubris, the British not only lost the battle, but also lost many soldiers, including Braddock himself. The Indians previously allied with the English switched their loyalties to the French, and Frederick County residents feared for their safety. When the legislature did not appropriate funds for a military company to defend this western outpost of the colony, Governor Horatio Sharpe ordered all Frederick County militia officers to meet him in Frederick Town. He proposed that "sixty to eighty men serve without pay and impress supplies wherever they could be found. Furthermore his proposal of building four forts in western Maryland through voluntary subscriptions was accepted and met by the citizens of Frederick County," according to Paul and Rita Gordon. Then, Governor Sharpe ordered the militias of Frederick, Prince George's, Baltimore, Cecil, Anne Arundel, Calvert, Charles, and St. Mary's Counties to meet in Frederick on October 10, 1755 and fan out to the western Maryland forts.

The next month, Frederick Town residents received the alarm that they faced attack from French and Indian fighters. Help was requested from Baltimore and Annapolis, and companies of volunteers arrived from Baltimore, but enemy forces only reached Emmitsburg. The war continued for seven more years, exacerbated by the refusal of the Proprietary government to provide substantial aid for protection. Families from western Frederick County moved through Frederick on their way east, fleeing in fear of Indian attack. The British eventually won the war and signed the Treaty of Paris in 1763. It was the formal ending, but the Indians continued to fight for nearly four more years.

The war exhausted the patience of backcountry settlers, angered that the Proprietary government wanted them to fight its wars but was not willing to put up the money to protect them. One example of this impatience was illustrated by Thomas Cresap, a frontier resident who assembled 60 riflemen in Frederick and threatened to take them to Annapolis to convince the legislature to allocate funds for frontier protection. This nonchalance on the part of British officials led to more than just impatience. Within two decades, the colonists would be in rebellion.

Chapter Two

A BASE OF REVOLUTIONARY FERVOR

(1760–1790s)

While continuing to build their community, Frederick Town residents joined the rest of the colonies in frustration with British rule. Frederick Town residents rebelled against taxes they believed to be oppressive, sent representatives to the Continental Congress, and fought in the Revolutionary War.

The root of this anger lay in the French and Indian War, which officially ended with the Treaty of Paris in 1763. England was saddled with a large war debt. The Crown believed that the colonists should pay for the war, and levied several taxes, most notably the Stamp Act, passed by Parliament in March 1765. The Stamp Act placed a tax on most legal documents, almanacs, newspapers, and playing cards, and required legal documents to be printed on special paper imprinted with a stamp. The colonists in Frederick Town believed these taxes added insult to injury. England would not send troops to protect the western outposts and now wanted to tax them to pay war debts.

Frederick Town and other colonial settlements used the "no taxation without representation" argument to protest the Stamp Act. Maryland and the rest of the colonies maintained that since they were not directly represented in Parliament, that body did not have the authority to tax them. In August, Frederick Town residents burned the stamp distributor in effigy. In October, Frederick County residents formed a local branch of the Sons of Liberty.

When the Stamp Act went into effect in November, demonstrations occurred in many cities. On November 23, the Frederick County court undertook what is believed to be the first official act of rebellion in the colonies. The justices declared that the court's business should proceed without the stamps, because Parliament had not properly notified the colonies of the Act by publishing it and because no stamps were available. Halting court business to await notice and official stamps would deprive citizens, the court reasoned. The court ordered the sheriff to take into custody the Court Clerk, John Darnall, for refusing to issue written legal decisions without the stamps. He was released when he agreed to submit to the ruling of the court.

The following Saturday, November 30, Frederick Town residents gave the Stamp Act a proper burial in an elaborate, melodramatic "funeral," described in the *Maryland Gazette* on December 16 and recorded by several local historians over the years. The funeral featured the colors of the Frederick Town military company, a banner, drums, and a coffin symbolizing the Stamp Act. The coffin carried this inscription, "The Stamp Act expired of a mortal stab received from the genius of liberty in Frederick

County Court, 23d November, 1765, Aged 22 days." The coffin also carried other inscriptions describing the colonists' frustrations with the British government, such as "Tyranny," "Soldiers quartered in private houses," and "military execution." The procession included an open chariot featuring an effigy of the Annapolis merchant Zachariah Hood, who the British Ministry appointed to distribute the stamps in Maryland. Hood was hated throughout the colony. The procession marched through the streets of Frederick Town and ended at a gallows at the courthouse square. There, someone read a satirical lamentation in the voice of the effigy of Hood mourning the deceased Stamp Act. The effigy stood by silently. The lamentation culminated in this request, "Let me be buried together with thee, and one grave receive our breathless remains! I hope, good people, you will not refuse this last request of a dying person. And, Oh! Oh! Oh!" At that very point, the effigy of Zachariah Hood himself "died," sinking down and tumbling out of the chariot. As he was falling, a member of the Sons of Liberty cried out, "Let him die like a dog!" The crowd cheered, and the drums played.

Mr. Hood's effigy was buried with the coffin. Then, the military company retired to the home of Mr. Samuel Swearingen for an "elegant supper" and a ball. In 1894, the Maryland General Assembly declared November 23 Repudiation Day. It was observed only in Frederick County and only as a bank half-holiday. Repudiation Day was listed in the *Maryland Manual,* the guide to state government, as recently as the 1987–1988 edition, but it does not appear after that year. However, in April 2001, the Frederick County Board of Education designated the day as worthy of recognition in classes.

Millard Milburn Rice, the historian who researched the early records of the Frederick County Court, offered two interesting observations about the court's repudiation of the Stamp Act. First, the court's order to proceed without stamps did not repudiate the Stamp Act itself, only the Court Clerk's refusal to issue legal papers without the stamps. At first, that fact seems to remove some of the order's significance. The lack of stamps made it convenient for the court to publicly declare that it would proceed without the stamps; the court never was tested on whether it would have issued the same opinion if stamps were available. However, in issuing the order, the court did take a more aggressive stance than other areas of Maryland. According to Rice, business in other parts of Maryland was at a standstill because of the lack of stamps. Business simply halted until the stamps arrived.

Rice's second observation makes the justices' decision seem more deliberate: The seemingly spontaneous order to ignore the Stamp Act might have been pre-planned and staged in a way to allow the Court Clerk, John Darnall, to save face with Proprietary and British officials. Darnall was a member of the "Proprietary establishment." He had served as Frederick County Court Clerk since the first session in 1748, and his father was Maryland attorney general. Darnall's son-in-law, James Dickson, was one of the court's 12 justices and might have requested that the planned Stamp Act protest be staged in a way that it appeared that his father-in-law was forced to participate. Since Darnall was ordered into the sheriff's custody unless he complied with the court's order, nobody could accuse him of being disloyal to the Crown.

Rice also believed that the repudiation was planned because the court's written order used more formal language than found in everyday opinions, and it suggests the influence of others beyond Frederick County, as evidenced by the use of the word "Province," referring to all of Maryland, instead of "county." The court should have been concerned with the lack of stamps in the county only, but instead, chose to state that "no stamps are yet arrived in this Province." Finally, the court's repudiation was issued five days into the November session, when it already had conducted much other routine business that, presumably, proceeded quietly without the stamps. The court chose a specific case, which it probably knew of in advance, to issue its opinion.

Paul Gordon, writing in the December 5, 2001 edition of *The Gazette*, described correspondence in the papers of Governor Sharpe indicating that it was commonly understood that the court acted purposefully. According to Gordon, Sharpe wrote in a letter that the Frederick County Court had "a case brought before them purposely as I understand, to make them act in violation of the stamp law."

The possibility that behind-the-scenes planning occurred makes the repudiation even more significant. Obviously, the extremely negative reaction to the Stamp Act extended more deeply than Parliament knew. Even the Provincial Court in Annapolis, the highest court in Maryland, ordered its clerk on March 31, 1766 to issue all papers and to transact all business without stamped paper. The damage to English commerce as a result of colonial opposition prompted Parliament to repeal the Stamp Act on March 18, 1766. News of the repeal did not reach the colonies until May 22.

Colonists' joy was short-lived, however. In November 1767, England imposed taxes on glass, paper, pasteboard, white and red lead, painters' colors, and tea imported into the colonies. Anti-importation societies formed in Frederick County and other areas of the colonies. These societies saw to it that colonists did not import or use any of the taxed items. For instance, in October 1769, several wagons loaded with prohibited goods arrived in Frederick from Pennsylvania, but delivery was not permitted. The drop in importation of taxed goods led to the infamous "Boston Tea Party" of 1773, in which opponents disguised as Indians boarded vessels of the East India Company docked in Boston Harbor and dumped tea overboard. Parliament closed Boston Harbor, and Frederick Town joined other colonial residents in solidarity against this act. Opposition to the British was becoming stronger and more organized.

Citizens of Frederick Town and other areas of the county met at the courthouse on May 20, 1774. The meeting's leader was John Hanson, who had moved to Frederick in 1773 and represented Frederick County in the Maryland Assembly. Hanson had an extensive history protesting British actions. He served in the Stamp Act Congress in 1765 and signed Maryland's non-importation agreement in 1769. Those assembled at the Frederick Town meeting resolved to oppose the closure of Boston Harbor and to work with the other colonies to stop all imports to and exports from England and the West Indies. They also resolved to send Hanson and eight other men to a general convention in Annapolis and named those nine and six others to a Committee of Correspondence authorized to send and to answer letters and to call general meetings in emergencies.

FREDERICK

The Continental Congress met in September, and two months later Frederick County citizens met again at the courthouse. They appointed a committee to oversee local efforts toward non-consumption and non-importation of British goods.

Meanwhile, Frederick Town and its institutions continued to grow. Craftsmen contributed to the city's physical growth, as documented by Reed and Burns in *In and Out of Frederick Town: Colonial Occupations*. Skilled carpenters known as housewrights designed and constructed buildings. They framed houses and completed the exterior work. Joiners focused on the interior finishes. They paneled walls, installed wood ceilings, and installed molding. They also made doors, windows, and shutters, and used manual lathes to make stairway balusters. Carpenters handled other work besides house construction. They built coffins, cabinets, stables, cow troughs, chicken coops, hog pens, and fences. They also did house repairs.

Frederick Town blacksmiths contributed their expertise to home construction. They provided tools to carpenters, joiners, and masons, and they made nails. They crafted heavy iron grates for bake ovens and fireplace cranes with trammels for holding kettles over the fire. Other products included meat spits, andirons, trivets, iron candlesticks, door hinges, drop latches, and bar locks. Blacksmiths made horseshoes for local horses and provided care for animals whose owners were passing through Frederick Town on the way west toward the mountains or east toward the Baltimore or Georgetown ports. In 1763, Francis Sanderson operated a similar business, a copper smithery, which made kettles, copper stills, pewter, lead instruments, and utensils.

In the leather trade, cordwainers made shoes. Shoemakers did the same but also repaired shoes. Both craftsmen made various types of shoes, but shoes for everyday wear featured leather closed with lace or a buckle and were attached to a wooden heel. All shoes were custom-made. Another type of leather worker was a saddler, who made harnesses, horse collars, bridles, and riding equipment, in addition to saddles. Some saddlers worked with other craftsmen to make wagons. Other leather specialists included leather breeches makers and tanners. Luckily for the rest of Frederick Town, Michael Raymer's tanyard was located downwind on the southeast side of town, on one of the easternmost Patrick Street lots near Carroll Creek.

The textile trade was one of the few that counted some women as members. Weavers sometimes hired women to spin wool and flax at home. Weavers used the resulting yarn to weave fabrics. Only a few women worked at looms in weaving shops. Typically, though, the weaver's customers brought their own wool and flax for him to weave into wool and linen fabric. Weavers dyed fabric that was faded and needed rejuvenating. Tailors made men's wear for summer and winter use in English patterns and moderately priced fabrics. A fashionable eighteenth-century suit resembled those seen in colonial paintings or other history books: breeches with knee buckles, matching hosiery, a shirt, a waistcoat, a long-sleeve coat, and a wool felt three-cornered hat. Men wore wigs, made of horse and goat hair, calf tails, and silk thread, but this practice ended after the Revolution. Seamstresses could not be documented before the Revolution, but it is possible that some unmarried women sewed at home to provide financial support for themselves.

A Base of Revolutionary Fervor

Colonial Frederick Town had several other occupations. One painter has been documented, David Biggle, who lived on East All Saints Street in 1764. It is not clear exactly what he did, whether house and furniture painting, sign painting, or painting portraits and pictures. Butchers not only sold meat but also killed and dressed the animals. By the time Frederick Town was established, the local butcher was shipping dry-cured meat to coastal cities for sale in Europe. Barrel and container makers, or coopers, were in heavy demand in Frederick Town. Residents stored many things in barrels and kegs, washed laundry and made sauerkraut in wooden tubs, and used wooden pails to transport water.

Merchants sold goods that local farmers and artisans could not fabricate. Local merchants obtained their products from coastal representatives of English merchants. Christopher Lowndes, a representative of Liverpool merchants John Hardman and William Whaley, maintained a store in Frederick Town. Some of the products local merchants stocked included tea, coffee, spices, sugar, pepper, molasses, ribbon, lace, buttons, buckles, snuff boxes, English textiles, knives, scissors, paper, compasses, tortoise shell combs, women's pumps and stockings, pewter spoons and bowls, and brass door hardware. Other merchants ran small businesses in a front room of their home. They bartered with their customers, who offered goods or services instead of cash to pay for their merchandise. The goods, such as dishes, deer skin, soap, candles, and tools, were resold to other customers. Lot 36 on the south side of East Patrick Street, two lots east of Market Street, is the only lot with a history of merchandising spanning 1764 to at least the 1980s.

One manufacturer was Robert Woods, who operated a wire mill in 1776. He also added a cotton and wool factory and a nail factory.

Fitting with Daniel Dulany's desire to build Frederick Town into a commercial center, a market house and town hall was built on two-and-a-half lots at the southeast corner of Market and Second Streets, which were acquired in 1768. Construction was financed by a public lottery. Market days were Wednesday and Saturday. "At Frederick Town's market house everyone with something to sell was a merchant on market days," according to Reed and Burns.

Frederick Town claimed a professional class. A few doctors hung their shingles here. They specialized as either physicians or chirurgeons (surgeons), but the majority probably were generalists. Medicine was very basic, by today's standards. Doctors made medicines from plants and minerals, used whiskey as anesthesia, and employed maggots to eat dead tissue. There is only sketchy information on chirurgeon Jacob Troutwine who practiced in the 1750s and Dr. James Brand who practiced in the late 1750s. Two doctors were more well-known. Dr. Adam Fisher, a chirurgeon, lived on North Market Street between Patrick and Church Streets in the 1760s and appears to have remained in town for at least several years. He was politically active on behalf of the Patriot cause. Dr. Philip Thomas, who arrived in Frederick Town in 1769, was educated at the College of Philadelphia, the first medical school in the colonies. Dr. Thomas lived on the southeast corner of Court and West Patrick Streets. He was well-respected during his 46 years in Frederick Town.

FREDERICK

Midwives numbered among the medical practitioners in colonial Frederick Town. These women, typically married or widowed, oversaw all births and treated mild illnesses or injuries. Midwives were trained by apprenticing with an experienced midwife, and made their own medicines.

No free schools, in the contemporary sense, existed in colonial Frederick Town, but a few teachers educated local children in private schools or as tutors. The German Reformed Church opened the first school in Frederick Town in 1747. Thomas Schley was the schoolmaster. Two schoolteachers came from Scotland, which they probably left because Presbyterians there were required to attend the Church of England in order to vote. John Ferguson lived on West Patrick Street across from the Reformed Church, where he might have taught. Andrew MacDonald taught the son of Joseph Doll, a Frederick Town merchant.

No full-time firefighters were employed, but volunteers organized a fire company in 1760. A lottery raised the $500 necessary to buy a fire engine.

In 1775, Frederick Town had 2,000 residents and was second only to Annapolis in size. Riders rode weekly posts for mail delivery to Baltimore and Winchester, Virginia. Most of Frederick Town's buildings were brick and stone, with a few wood structures. More than 340 lots were established by 1782. As the town grew, gradations in income and status developed. The most prominent residents lived in stately houses built around the courthouse square. Behind these mansions were located the quarters of the town's least prominent residents, slaves.

"Most of the prominent families in Frederick, white families, had slaves," according to Kathleen Snowden, a writer and historian interviewed for the 1997 documentary of Frederick County's African-American history, *Up From the Meadows*. Those families included Thomas Johnson, Maryland's first governor, and General John Ross Key, the father of "Star Spangled Banner" writer Francis Scott Key. According to Snowden's examination of Underground Railroad records, Johnson's wife Ann was a particularly cruel master. Apparently, she sold two children because she was angry with their mother, who was one of her slaves.

By the end of 1774, Frederick Town residents joined the rest of the colonies in taking more dramatic action against Britain. On December 8, Frederick residents met to organize a militia of all men between 16 and 50 years old, and to affirm the need to now turn to local industries for goods and services and to become commercially and financially independent of England. The colonists also took action to form their own governing bodies. Like the counties in the rest of the province, Frederick County residents in January 1775 formed a Committee of Observation to act as a local government and represent them at the Continental Congress and the Provincial Convention. The committee operated for two years, until Maryland became a state in 1777. On June 15, 1775, Thomas Johnson, who was serving in the Continental Congress and possibly was living in Frederick Town by this time, had the honor of nominating his friend Colonel George Washington to be commander in chief of the Continental Army.

Two days later was the Battle of Bunker Hill, and in the words of historian J. Thomas Scharf, "from this hour the colonists were fully roused. In Maryland all was vigilance and activity." No fighting occurred in or near Frederick County, but the war affected the daily lives of residents. Men from the city and the county went off to fight. The first group of men sent to war were members of two rifle companies. Each company consisted of a captain, three lieutenants, four sergeants, four corporals, a drummer, and 68 privates. They agreed to serve for a year at a monthly pay rate ranging from $20 for the captain to $6.66 for the privates. They were required to provide their own arms and clothes. Throughout the war, troops obtained their weapons from the gunlock manufactory established in 1776 on the corner of All Saints and Carroll Streets. This manufactory provided arms to Frederick County troops.

Once again, as it had all too recently during the previous war, Frederick and the vicinity faced danger from the frontier. Virginia Governor Dunmore, who was trying to maintain British authority in that colony, devised an elaborate plan to divide the northern and southern colonies and thus stop the Revolution. He enlisted Dr. John Connolly of Lancaster, Pennsylvania, to assemble an army of Indians at Detroit who would seize Pittsburgh and then invade western Maryland and Virginia. The force would establish a post at Cumberland in western Frederick County, and then move to Alexandria, Virginia, where Governor Dunmore would meet them with a fleet and a group of runaway slaves. Unfortunately for Connolly, he and three others were spotted near Hagerstown, recognized as British Loyalists, and brought to Frederick. In late 1775, they were held prisoner in the third floor of a home on Second Street for seven weeks until their trial in Philadelphia. The danger of skirmishes on the frontier continued to plague Frederick and the vicinity throughout the war.

Frederick's interior location made it a favored site to store military supplies. Gunpowder was brought to Frederick Town from Annapolis to ensure that it would not fall into British hands, should the capital be attacked. The gunpowder was stored in the market house. Military stores at Annapolis were moved to Frederick again in 1777.

On June 7, 1776, the Continental Congress voted to end the allegiance of the colonies to England. Frederick County residents voted 10 days later to support that decision. Noting the danger of their decision, Frederick Town residents pledged their support "at the hazard of our lives and fortunes." Congress adopted the Declaration of Independence a month later, on July 4. A state convention, which included Thomas Johnson, had adopted Maryland's state constitution a year earlier in 1775. The State Assembly met in February 1777 and elected Johnson governor.

One of the most visible effects of the war on Frederick Town was the presence of prisoners of war, troops, and others who used the town as a crossroads. Thomas Jefferson passed through Frederick Town in 1776 while on his way to the Continental Congress. His memorandum book contains an entry for dinner and lodging at "Crush's in Frederick Town," probably the West Patrick Street inn of Catherine Grosh Kimball. The first prisoners were brought to Frederick Town in May 1776. In late December 1777, 100 more prisoners were housed here temporarily while Fort Frederick, in western Maryland, was readied. Frederick Town's permanent barracks, known as the Hessian Barracks, were completed in 1778. The original purpose of the barracks as directed by the State Assembly was to quarter soldiers. The complex also held British and German prisoners captured at Saratoga, Trenton, and Yorktown. The prisoners lived in the barracks and 100 huts on the grounds. About 1,000 colonial troops passed through Frederick Town on May 31, 1781 en route to Virginia to meet General LaFayette.

The German prisoners felt comfortable in Frederick because so many residents still maintained their German culture. Congress sought to encourage the Germans to remain and settle, so the prisoners were allowed to be mobile and hire themselves out to local farmers, many of whom were German. Many former Hessian soldiers stayed, bought farms, and married local women.

British Loyalists again attempted to undermine the Revolution, this time by attempting to free British prisoners held in Maryland and Virginia. Seven Loyalists were brought to Frederick in 1780 to answer a charge of high treason for their roles in the plot. Four were pardoned, on the condition that they remain in England for the rest of the war. Three were executed, including Casper Fritchie, whose son later married Civil War figure Barbara Fritchie. The traitors were hung, drawn, and quartered, a particularly gruesome, medieval punishment that was based in English common law. The punishment was meant to be a deterrent for anyone else contemplating treasonous activities.

Further action was taken against Maryland Tories in October 1780, when the legislature voted to confiscate all property of British subjects who had left the state unless they returned by March 1782 and took the oath of allegiance. Daniel Dulany III—a Loyalist whose grandfather laid out Frederick Town—lost his extensive land holdings in western Maryland and ground rents on the lots he owned in Frederick because he moved to England at the beginning of the war. Many people suspected of Tory loyalties were required to take the oath of allegiance to the State of Maryland.

Residents erupted in joy when the war ended. A German officer organized a fireworks celebration, and a German band played music at a ball Frederick Town held to celebrate the war's end. The Treaty of Paris was signed in September 1783, and the Continental Congress ratified it on January 14, 1784.

Active in Revolutionary politics, Thomas Johnson and John Hanson continued to serve Maryland and the new country. Johnson, who led 1,800 men as 1st Brigadier General of Maryland's militia in New Jersey, accepted the job of Maryland's first governor. He served a one-year term and was elected two more times. He was re-elected to Congress in 1780 and also served again in the state legislature. Johnson encouraged Maryland's representatives to vote in favor of the Articles of Confederation before its ratification in 1781, as long as other colonies rescinded their rights to lands west of the Alleghenies. Johnson was associate justice of the Supreme Court from 1791 to 1793, and resigned because of ill health. Johnson's old friend, now President Washington, asked him to be secretary of state, but ill health again forced him to decline. Johnson's last public appearance was in 1800; he died in 1819 at Rose Hill Manor, the estate built in the 1790s by his son-in-law on land Johnson bought for his daughter as a wedding gift in February 1776. Rose Hill is a public museum located off North Market Street north of Sixteenth Street.

A Base of Revolutionary Fervor

John Hanson was a signer of the Articles of Confederation. He joined the other delegates in demanding that the other colonies give up their rights to western lands. Under the Articles, Hanson was elected first president of Congress in 1781, which to some historians means that he technically was the first president of the United States (the current executive branch was not created until established by the Constitution in 1789). Hanson only served a one-year term and died a short time later in 1783, at Oxon Hill, in Prince George's County.

Once again, Frederick Town residents turned their attention to improving the town. To start, they only had to look out their front doors to the city streets. *Pictorial History of Frederick, Maryland* described the conditions this way:

> The streets were badly graded and unpaved, and there was little drainage. Dry weather produced blinding dust, and wet weather produced deep quagmires of mud. Dead animals often rotted in the streets; the town had no provision for regular garbage removal. There was little in the way of street lighting once public and private dwellings had dashed their lights, usually around nine o'clock.

A commission was established in 1786 to tax residents to raise funds to address these problems. Funding took a while because taxes needed to be kept at affordable levels. These conditions were common in many towns, and they allowed disease to flourish. Frederick Town residents were concerned in 1793 over an epidemic of yellow fever in Philadelphia that was believed to have been brought there by refugees from San Domingo. Frederick Town residents formed patrols to prohibit people and products from Philadelphia from entering the town.

Mathias Bartgis began publication of the *Maryland Chronicle,* the first recorded newspaper in Frederick County, in 1786. Bartgis brought his printing press to Frederick Town in 1779, but did not begin publishing for seven more years. His newspaper also was published as the *Universal Advertiser.* It was the first newspaper published in Maryland west of Baltimore, and it appeared in both German and English. Its original subscription list of 150 received weekly newspapers on Wednesday via a newsboy on horseback. The newspaper was renamed in 1792 the *Maryland Gazette* or the *Frederick County Advertiser*, and renamed again in 1794 the *Federal Gazette*. In 1801, the name changed once again to the *Republican Gazette*, and the paper became heavily political.

Two other newspapers operated in Frederick Town during the late eighteenth century. John Winter, a printer and schoolteacher with Federalist leanings, produced *Rights of Man* from 1790 to 1802. Dr. John D. Cary published *The Key* from 1798 to 1800.

News was also carried by private postal and stage line services. In 1786, Bartgis started a subscription post service between Baltimore, Frederick Town, Hagerstown, and Sharpsburg. Another post service advertised in 1797 offered deliveries to Lancaster and Philadelphia. Stage services advertised in the 1790s took passengers to Georgetown, Baltimore, Lancaster, and York. These services used taverns as terminals; patrons were informed of schedules through advertisements that told readers at which tavern to meet the post rider or stagedriver, and on which dates and times.

FREDERICK

Milling began as an industry in Frederick Town in the late 1700s. One of the first flour mills in Frederick County and the first structure on present-day Bentz Street was Old Town Mill, built by Jacob Bentz in the late 1700s. The mill was located just north of Carroll Creek, on the west side of Bentz between Church and Second Streets. The mill was powered by a millrace that extended from a point on the creek about a mile west, to provide enough grade variations so that gravity could power the mill's wheel. The building's front included a 1787 date stone, but some historians believe that it might have been older. Bentz acquired the property from the sale of Daniel Dulany's confiscated lands. The property changed hands several times, and in 1895 it was purchased by Newton Zentz, earning it the name Zentz mill. The mill burned down in 1928, and the land later became part of Baker Park.

Also during this period, a warehouse was constructed that later played a role in the city's tanning industry that flourished in the nineteenth century. The three-story warehouse was built in 1797 by Dr. William S. Bantz on Brewer's Alley, which today is Court Street from Patrick Street to South Street. Gideon Bantz, a nineteenth-century businessman, judge, politician, and civic leader, later owned and operated this building as part of the city's tanning industry.

Several private schools operated in Frederick Town from its founding, but Frederick Town's first "free" school was not opened until 1797. Frederick Academy was built on a half-acre of land at Record and Council Streets. The school was a long time coming. Upon Frederick County's creation in 1748, the county was subject to the 1723 law requiring a school in each county of Maryland. A school was not specifically directed to be built in Frederick County until 1763, when a provincial law appointed seven men to be trustees of the Frederick County Free School and to obtain an acre in Frederick Town to build the school. No school was built, and a second law in 1768 changed the trustees and directed that a half-acre be bought for the school. The General Assembly declared the school Frederick County's free school in 1796.

More churches were built. The Presbyterian Church was established in Frederick in 1780 at the corner of Fourth and Bentz Streets. One of the significant early pastors was Dr. Samuel Knox, who was the first principal of Frederick Academy and also a friend of Thomas Jefferson. The congregation relocated to West Second Street, where it built a new church, in 1827. Baptists also were meeting in Frederick, as evidenced by a covenant they signed in 1790 agreeing to adhere to the tenets of the faith. The congregation counted a few African Americans among its membership. Although Methodists were present in Frederick during the Colonial period, the denomination did not build its first church in town until 1792, on West Church Street. The church was enlarged in 1806 and 1828, and a new church was built on East Church Street in 1840.

Amusements returned to Frederick Town after the Revolutionary War. Bartgis's newspaper carried several announcements of plays and other performances. In May 1786 the Frederick Town Theatre presented the tragedy "The Revenge" by a Dr. Young and a farce called "The Mock Doctor." The company of actors performed Wednesdays and Fridays for two weeks. In August 1786, the Market House hosted a performance of Voltaire's "Zara." French dancers performed on the tightrope in June 1792.

A Base of Revolutionary Fervor

An event that generated great excitement was President George Washington's visit to Frederick Town in the early 1790s on his way to Philadelphia. A company of horsemen met the President south of Frederick Town and accompanied him north through town up Market Street to the home of his friend, Thomas Johnson. Reportedly, a young Barbara Fritchie, at that time Barbara Hauer, served coffee to the President at a local tavern, but some researchers question whether this actually happened. "That night, the town was illuminated," according to the historian T.J.C. Williams, and the townspeople treated Washington "with marks of high respect and great affection." The citizens showered praise on him in an address. Washington responded in a letter thanking Frederick Town for its role in creating the new nation, and he wished the citizens luck for the future.

Frederick Town residents again faced danger before the end of the eighteenth century. The Whiskey Rebellion began in 1794 when farmers in western Pennsylvania refused to pay the Federal tax on corn liquor levied by Congress in 1791. Farmers were upset because they used corn whiskey as currency. Representatives sent by President Washington to collect the tax in 1794 met armed resistance. In August, Washington ordered the rebels to disperse and requested that the governors of Maryland, Virginia, Pennsylvania, and New Jersey form a militia of 15,000 men. Meanwhile, in Frederick, those who were exempt from military duty met on September 6 to form a company to protect the city in the event that the rebellion spread south. Their action was timely, for several days later Maryland Governor Thomas Sim Lee received a report that insurgents had assembled in Cumberland, in western Maryland, and were preparing to storm Frederick to steal arms from the state arsenal. By September 19, troops from Baltimore, Georgetown, southern Maryland, and Frederick were assembled in town. Troops met at Cumberland, and the rebels fled.

The Whiskey Rebellion was thwarted, but for a third time Frederick Town residents were forced to take up arms and face the threat of military activity. They would be required to make this sacrifice twice more in the next century.

Chapter Three

FREDERICK IN THE NEW NATION

(1790s–1840s)

As the nineteenth century dawned, Frederick Town was a growing town on the frontier with thriving industries. The town continued to be an actor in the new nation.

In 1798, 2,606 people lived in 449 dwellings in Frederick Town. The population comprised 2,300 whites and 306 blacks, most of whom were enslaved. Seven religious denominations were active in Frederick: Roman Catholic, Episcopal, Lutheran, German Presbyterian or Calvinist, Presbyterian, Baptist, and Methodist. Public buildings included a poorhouse, a courthouse, the county schoolhouse, and two market houses, all of which were brick construction. A stone jail contained a large yard surrounded by a stone wall.

The thriving town supported many occupations, including tobacconists, blacksmiths, saddlers, joiners, comb-makers, shoemakers, weavers, wagon-makers, tavern owners, hatters, stocking weavers, gunsmiths, nailers, tailors, shopkeepers and merchants, painters, masons, skinners, tanners, curriers, printers, butchers, clock and watch makers, silversmiths, coppersmiths, wheelwrights, chair makers, harness makers, potters, makers of breeches and gloves, apothecaries, brewers, barbers, cabinet makers, pump makers, brickmakers, brushmakers, bakers, carpenters, coopers, distillers, millers, heel makers, plasterers, teachers, doctors, and lawyers. From this list, it appeared that residents could obtain most any good or service locally.

Five years later, the man who led the 1803 expedition to the interior of the new nation on behalf of President Thomas Jefferson stopped in Frederick to prepare for and begin his trip. Meriwether Lewis arrived in Frederick Town in April 1803 to buy supplies in preparation for the Corps of Discovery's exploration of the Louisiana Purchase. Lewis first arrived in the area in March 1803, and stopped first in Harper's Ferry, Virginia to obtain arms and other supplies at the federal armory and to oversee construction of a large collapsible iron boat frame for the trip. A month later, on April 15, he arrived in Frederick. He appears to have used the town as a base of operations to make arrangements to obtain supplies in the region, including Philadelphia and Pittsburgh. According to historians Dean Herrin and Teresa S. Moyer, Lewis wrote General William Irvine, the superintendent of military stores in Philadelphia, to request 193 pounds of "Portable-Soup," which was a "dried soup of various beans and vegetables." Soon afterward, Lewis left Frederick for Lancaster and Philadelphia to buy supplies and receive scientific training.

After Lewis left Washington, D.C. on July 5 to begin the expedition, he spent the first night of his journey in Frederick. While here, he arranged for a teamster to pick up supplies waiting for him in Harper's Ferry and to transport them to Pittsburgh. When the teamster failed, Lewis had to find another local teamster. Some believe Lewis also might have come here to acquire supplies from the Hessian Barracks, one of the state's armories. However, according to Herrin and Moyer:

> no evidence has surfaced in any of the letters and documents associated with the Lewis and Clark journey that Lewis obtained supplies from the Barracks. Detailed lists have survived of supplies acquired in Harpers Ferry and Philadelphia, leaving one to assume a similar list would exist if supplies had been obtained in Frederick.

Lewis did receive help in Frederick from Lieutenant Colonel Thomas H. Cushing, the U.S. Army's Adjutant and Inspector, who was headquartered here. Cushing arranged for eight recruits from the military post in Carlisle, Pennsylvania, to accompany Lewis from Pittsburgh to St. Louis. Although the town did not play a primary role, Frederick and its resources helped support the expedition, which was significant in this country's history.

Frederick Town once again acted as a crossroads for the Lewis and Clark expedition when a delegation of Osage Indians, sent by Lewis to Washington to meet President Jefferson, arrived in Frederick a year later, on July 9, 1804. The delegation's leader was Payouska, Chief of the Great Osages. According to a local newspaper, the *Hornet*, the group comprised a "King," eleven chiefs, and two boys. The group stayed at Jacob Miller's tavern. The *Hornet* and two other newspapers, the *Republican Advocate* and the *Frederick-Town Herald*, were full of descriptions of the men. The men were tall, above six feet, wearing the dress of white people but bald except for tufts of hair, adorned with silver ornaments, on the crowns of their heads. An interpreter accompanying the group, Jean Pierre Chouteau, carried specimens from the expedition, including a horned toad, ore samples, salt, and a map, to present to President Jefferson.

In 1801 the growing town attracted two young lawyers. Francis Scott Key, who wrote the "Star Spangled Banner," and Roger Brooke Taney, who later served as Chief Justice of the Supreme Court when it issued its Dred Scott Decision that slaves were not citizens, moved to Frederick. Key and Taney met while students at St. John's College in Annapolis, and became brothers-in-law when Taney married Key's sister, Anne. Taney and Key might have practiced law together for several years at an office on Court Street north of Patrick Street. Neither was born in Frederick, and both are remembered for acts that occurred after their residence here, but both are buried here, and the city claims both men as its own.

Key was born in 1779 at Terra Rubra, an estate located in a portion of northern Frederick County that is now Carroll County. He graduated from St. John's and then remained in Annapolis to study law in the office of his uncle, Philip Barton Key. Key left Annapolis and came to Frederick in 1801 to practice law. He left just four years later to go to Georgetown. He was appointed U.S. district attorney. He was known for his friendship and counsel to President Andrew Jackson, and for his support of an organization he helped found to send blacks back to Africa. Key is most known for writing "The Star Spangled Banner" in 1814 while moved at the sight of the United States flag, which was still flying after the British bombardment of Fort McHenry in Baltimore during the War of 1812.

Key witnessed the bombardment while trying to win the release of his friend, Dr. William Beanes, who had been arrested by the British for instigating residents of the Prince George's County town of Marlborough to capture British troops retreating from Washington, D.C. during the war. With the approval of President James Madison, Key traveled to the mouth of the Potomac River, where the British fleet was preparing to head north to attack Fort McHenry, which guarded the Patapsco River entrance to Baltimore. With Key was John Skinner, the U.S. representative for the exchange of prisoners. British Admiral Alexander Cochrane agreed to Beanes's release persuaded by letters from the captured British troops attesting to their humane treatment. Cochrane detained Key and Skinner with the British fleet until the attack on Fort McHenry concluded.

The night the bombardment started, Key and Skinner were in a position to see the 30- by 42-foot United States flag flying above the fort. The sound of the explosions guaranteed that the fort had not surrendered, but when the noise stopped, they anxiously paced the deck, awaiting daybreak so they could see whether the flag still flew. As the now-famous song goes, "by the dawn's early light" they could see that "our flag was still there." When he saw the flag and the retreating British troops, Key was inspired to jot down some lines on the back of a letter he had in his pocket. Key was not just a lawyer but also a poet and hymn writer. He intended for the song to be sung to the melody of the popular British drinking song, "To Anacreon in Heaven." Key refined the song in his Baltimore hotel room that night and showed it to his brother-in-law, Captain Joseph Nicholson, who had helped defend Fort McHenry. Nicholson was so impressed that he had the song printed and distributed on handbills. A Baltimore newspaper printed the song a few days later on September 20, 1814.

Key died of pneumonia on January 11, 1843, at the age of 63, while visiting his daughter in Baltimore. His remains were moved to Mount Olivet Cemetery in 1866, and in 1898 his remains and those of his wife, Mary Taylor Lloyd, were buried in the base of a monument unveiled on August 8. The navy began playing Key's poem at morning flag-raising ceremonies in 1889. It became the official anthem of the armed forces in 1916, and Congress made the song the country's national anthem in 1931.

Roger Brooke Taney resided in Frederick for 18 years after the 1805 departure of his friend and brother-in-law, Key. Taney, originally from Calvert County, decided to move to Frederick in 1801 after losing a campaign for re-election to the Maryland General Assembly. He was attracted to Frederick because several other young friends from his Annapolis days lived here, including Key. Also, he thought he could succeed as a young lawyer in the Frederick County bar. The bar itself was only 53 years old at that point, young compared to those in the more established counties of Maryland, and most of the lawyers were only a few years older than Taney. Taney married Anne Key, Francis Scott Key's sister, in 1806, and the couple and their daughters might have lived in a house on South Bentz Street. In addition to practicing law, Taney also was a director of the Frederick County Bank and a trustee of the Frederick Academy.

One of Taney's significant legal cases during his practice in Frederick was his 1811 co-defense of Army Brigadier General James Wilkinson. The trial was held in Frederick at the barracks. Wilkinson was a Frederick County resident accused of several acts of treason, including conspiring with former Vice President Aaron Burr to establish a western empire between the Ohio River and Mexico. Taney and another attorney, John Hanson Thomas, took the case, even though the two lawyers believed at first that Wilkinson was guilty and betrayed Burr to protect himself. They later changed their minds and accepted no fee. Through Taney's and Thomas's efforts during the three-month trial, Wilkinson was acquitted and restored to military service.

Taney is best remembered for his state and national service, which occurred after he moved from Frederick to Baltimore in 1823. Taney was appointed Maryland attorney general in 1827. President Andrew Jackson named him U.S. attorney general in 1831 and then secretary of the treasury in 1833. Taney was confirmed as an associate justice of the Supreme Court in 1836. Taney's most controversial action came in the 1857 Dred Scott Decision, which declared that blacks were not citizens and thus could not sue in federal court, and also that Congress had no authority to regulate slavery in the territories. The decision resulted from the appeal of Dred Scott, who sued his owner's wife for his freedom after the owner died. Scott claimed he was free because he had lived with his owner, an army surgeon, in Wisconsin Territory and Illinois, where slavery was illegal. Taney, at this point the chief justice, wrote and delivered the majority opinion, which galvanized anti-slavery advocates and helped bring on the Civil War. Taney died in 1864 at the age of 87, and was buried in St. John's Cemetery on East Fourth Street. He remains a controversial figure.

Once again, as it had only 20 years earlier, war intruded on the lives of Frederick Town residents, during the War of 1812 against the British. Frederick Town was not in danger, but the city was a crossroads for military activity. Men who signed up for service at the Frederick Town recruiting office were paid $5 a month, as well as a "signing bonus" of $16 and the promise of three months' pay and 160 acres if they won an honorable discharge. Troops were quartered in the barracks and traveled through Frederick Town en route to the theaters of war in Washington and Baltimore. After Washington fell in 1814, 3,000 troops passed through town. More than 100 British prisoners were marched from Washington and held in Frederick Town. A British spy was captured in Frederick Town when an officer recognized him as a British soldier.

Since Frederick Town was removed from the fighting, it was a good place to store valuables from Baltimore and Washington. Thirteen wagons carried money from Baltimore to Frederick Town for safekeeping, and wagons brought public archives and documents from Washington.

U.S. forces invaded Canada in October 1814, and Frederick Town joined the rest of the country in celebrating the victory. Church bells rang, and a nighttime torch procession lit up the town. The war ended two months later with the Treaty of Ghent.

FREDERICK

Despite the intrusion of the War of 1812, the early nineteenth century was a time of growth and development for Frederick Town. Daily life became easier as infrastructure was improved through better transportation, piped water, nighttime lighting, and fire protection services. Local industries thrived, and residents continued to build such community institutions as banks, schools, and churches.

One dramatic sign that both Frederick and the country were growing was the construction of the route that eventually became part of the National Road. This road extended from Baltimore through Frederick to Vandalia, Illinois. Later, this road was designated part of U.S. Route 40, and extended to California. The portion that passed through Frederick was the vision of the Baltimore and Frederick Turnpike Company, which was chartered by the state legislature in 1805 to build a turnpike from Baltimore to Boonsboro, located west of Frederick. With the construction of these roads that brought visitors from east and west, Frederick became a crossroads as never before.

In 1815, the Maryland General Assembly authorized the extension of the turnpike from Boonsboro to Hagerstown, and in 1819 the road was extended further to Cumberland. From there, the road linked to the first interstate road authorized by Congress, the National Road, also called the National Pike. Congress had approved construction of that road from Cumberland to the Ohio River in 1806. The Baltimore to Frederick turnpike and the other roads leading to Cumberland were incorporated into the National Road. The National Road eventually was extended west through Ohio, Indiana, and Illinois.

The construction of the turnpike brought direct and indirect benefits to Frederick. Farmers, merchants, and others who needed to transport goods on the 45-mile route between Frederick and Baltimore could do so more cheaply and more quickly, and on a better-quality macadam road than the original dirt road. Wagons transported flour, whiskey, and other products for sale to Baltimore, and returned with merchandise for sale by merchants in Frederick and other western Maryland towns. This road also brought many travelers through Frederick who changed their horses and enjoyed food and lodging at taverns and inns, such as the Old Stone Tavern at the corner of Patrick and present-day Jefferson Streets. Visitors to this tavern included Henry Clay, Andrew Jackson, and Daniel Webster. In 1825, nineteen public houses offered entertainment, food, and lodging in Frederick Town.

The road's users included large eastbound wagons drawn by six horses and equipped with rear wheels 10 feet high. They stopped in Frederick to sell products transported from the west and loaded their wagons with flour from Frederick to sell to eastern markets. On return trips, they carried groceries and dry goods to be sold at points west of Frederick. Mail carriers on horseback also used the road and stopped at taverns to deposit the mail and change horses.

"The days of the old National Pike were the romantic times of the County," according to T.J.C. Williams in *History of Frederick County Maryland*:

> Coaches dashed through at the rate of twelve miles an hour, and wagons
> followed each other so closely that it was said with some pardonable

exaggeration that the heads of one team were in the rear of the wagon before it. There were many private carriages, many travelers on horseback, and an endless procession of cattle and sheep from the rich pastures of what was then called the West. Along the road every few miles, was a tavern and the reputation of the meals served in them, the venison, the bearsteaks, the hot bread, the ham and eggs, the whiskey has lost nothing from the lapse of time.

These visitors added energy to Frederick. Horns announced the arrival of the stage and the mail, and all the wagons, visitors, and animals passing through undoubtedly added to the din.

Two local landmarks serve as evidence of Frederick's status as a stop on the National Road. The jug bridge monument was part of a stone bridge built in 1808 to transport the turnpike across the Monocacy River. Frederick County stonemason Leonard Harbaugh built the bridge for $55,000. Next to the bridge, Harbaugh built the monument, which resembles a large jug. The bridge lasted 134 years, collapsing into the river in 1942. The jug monument was moved to its current location at Bowman Farm Road and East Patrick Street. The other landmark is a milestone on the northeast corner of Patrick Street and Maxwell Avenue. The elements and time have eroded it, but when it was installed around 1820 it had a notation that indicated to travelers that Baltimore was 45 miles away. Other milestones are located along the road elsewhere in the county.

Frederick citizens also made local road improvements. For instance, Market Street was paved in 1811 with money raised in a lottery. Eight thousand tickets were sold at $5 apiece.

In December 1816, the Maryland General Assembly passed an act incorporating the city as Frederick. The act officially dropped the "Town" from the city's name. The incorporation act also called for the election of a mayor and five aldermen to serve three-year terms, and for the division of the city into seven wards that each would elect one council member to serve a year. So, the early municipal governing bodies had both aldermen and councilmen, 12 people total, until 1878 when the state legislature abolished the council and gave full governing power to the aldermen. The first municipal election in Frederick was held on the last Monday of February in 1817. The municipal government replaced the Board of Commissioners that had governed Frederick since 1787. Some of the early offices are familiar and some served needs that are now obsolete. For instance, Frederick still has a mayor but no longer employs a flour inspector or a town weigher.

Also around this time, Frederick received other modern conveniences. By 1818, three fire companies were formed. Friendship Fire Company formed in 1807, and the company purchased an engine from London. The Union Fire Company was formed during this time period and was in existence in 1813. Independent Fire Company was formed in 1818 and is the only one of these three still in existence. Independent first was established on West Church Street one door west of present-day Trinity Chapel, and now is located on Baughmans Lane south of Rosemont Avenue. Two later fire companies that survived are Junior Fire Company, which formed in 1838 and built an engine house on North Market Street in 1846, and United Fire Company, which organized in 1845 and built a station house on South Market Street.

The first water works was installed in 1825, when a water company was organized at a meeting at Talbott's Hotel. The water came from a spring 2.5 miles northwest of Frederick, through wooden pipes, and to a reservoir a mile from Frederick. The water then was distributed from the reservoir. By 1839, this system was deemed inadequate. Funds were raised through a lottery and two loans, and a new system was completed in November 1845 for $90,000. Ordinances set rates for water use. Later, the city dug artesian wells to provide water.

The streets were not lit until 1832. Before that time, travelers negotiated the muddy streets using light from either their own lanterns or the lamps that illuminated the homes or shops until bedtime, which then was at an early hour. An ordinance passed in April provided 36 street lamps, but they were only lit on moonless nights. Gas light arrived in 1853. Pipes were laid in 1849, and in 1850 the city entered into a contract with a gas company to provide gas for street lights. In January 1853 an ordinance authorized erecting 35 iron lamp posts at a cost of $19 each. The ordinance required that the gas cost no more than $25 a year for each post, and also specified the maximum size of the burners. The lights were not entirely welcomed by some concerned about cost, but the naysayers were "denounced as loving darkness rather than light." This might have been a reference to the existence of crime and disorderly conduct after dark.

Local industries continued to develop. John Kimmerly and Nicholas Hoover operated a rope factory on Patrick Street in 1809. M.A. Miller was the first candy maker in Frederick. He opened his shop in 1812, on a lot on the north side of the first block of West Patrick Street. A Mrs. Getz opened a bakery in 1822 and was the first person in town to sell ice cream. A carpet factory was established in 1833.

Tanning was a major industry in Frederick. Tanneries had been operating since the mid-1700s and had their heyday in the 1800s. The businesses operated along Carroll Creek, making use of waterpower. They were located mainly in southeastern Frederick so that the prevailing west to east winds did not blow the tanneries' stench throughout the town. Eight tanneries operated in Frederick Town in 1810, according to the census of that year. In the 1830s, the two largest tanneries were operated by Valentine Birely, who was located on the west side of Carroll Street north of Carroll Creek, and Gideon Bantz, who operated his tannery in the former warehouse on Court Street discussed in Chapter Two. By 1850, Frederick had 11 tanneries. An 1853 map of Frederick depicted six tanning yards along the creek. By 1888, only four tanneries operated in Frederick.

Although water from Carroll Creek also could have powered mills, not many seem to have operated along the creek. Jacob Bentz's Old Town Mill on Bentz Street, which ground grain, was the only mill operating in 1808 according to a map of that year. According to the 1853 map, that mill remained the only one. Another mill, known first as Gambrill Mill and the Mountain City Mill, began operating on Carroll Street after the Civil War.

Another sign of Frederick's growth and prosperity was the formation of banks. Several banks were begun as branches of banks in other cities in Maryland. The first bank established in Frederick was Central National Bank, a branch of the Farmers' Bank of Maryland in Annapolis. The branch became so successful that it broke away from Farmers' Bank and obtained a charter as Central Bank of Frederick in 1854. The second bank to begin operations in Frederick was Farmers and Mechanics National Bank, a branch of the Bank of Westminster. Farmers and Mechanics began service in 1817 in a room of Creager's Tavern on Market and Second Streets, where the bank eventually located. The next year, the Frederick County National Bank began operations as a state bank. In 1828, the Fredericktown Savings Institution opened in the spare room of a doctor's office. Successors to the latter three banks are still operating today.

Frederick residents continued to build two other important community institutions: schools and churches. The Catholic Church was responsible for three of the schools in Frederick. The school that became Visitation Academy began in 1824 when five Catholic nuns from the Sisters of Charity religious order arrived from Emmitsburg to start a convent and school. The pastor of St. John's, Father John McElroy, had negotiated with the superiors of the order the previous year to establish a community in Frederick. The nuns lived in a dilapidated old two-room log dwelling located on the site of the present school, at 200 E. Second Street. Despite the rustic accommodations, the sisters pressed on with their school, placing an ad in local newspapers stating that the St. John's Female Benevolent and Frederick Free School would open and that all denominations would be welcome. The school was a success, and the next year a larger structure was built on the site for the school and an orphanage. The Sisters of Charity left the school in 1846 and were replaced by the Sisters of the Visitation, who gave the school its present name. The Catholic Church also established a school for boys, St. John's Literary Institute, in 1829.

Frederick Academy received a charter from the Maryland General Assembly changing its name to Frederick College in 1830. It was still a free school in 1910, according to T.J.C. Williams in *History of Frederick County, Maryland*, who said of the school, "Ministers and missionaries, physicians and lawyers, merchants and farmers have here secured at no cost to them, the education and training that gave them their place in the world." The school building, at Record and Council Streets, was demolished in 1936 to widen Record Street and to build the C. Burr Artz Library.

The Jesuits established a third Catholic school during this period in 1833, the Jesuit Novitiate, which trained priests. This was not a new school but the relocation to Frederick of a school that had been established in White Marsh. The Novitiate was established on the grounds of the former church on the northwest corner of Second and Chapel, which was expanded to accommodate the students. The building was torn down in 1903.

The Frederick Female Seminary, another school for girls, was established in 1839. Hiram Winchester came to Frederick in 1830 and opened the school on North Market Street. Winchester erected two ornate classical buildings on East Church Street and relocated the school to these buildings in 1845. In 1893 the seminary became the Woman's College, and in 1913 the college moved to the northwest side of the city and was renamed Hood College. The original seminary buildings are called Winchester Hall in honor of their builder, and today house Frederick County government.

The city's first three public schools were built in this period, corresponding to the statewide movement to establish more public schools. In 1823, the General Assembly created the offices of superintendent and school commissioners, and other structures related to a school system. In 1826, Frederick County voters approved a primary school system, but as of 1846 students were still being assessed a fee for their schooling, in addition to the county and state contribution. It was not until 1872 that state laws formed the basis for the current school system supported by taxation.

Not much information is available about these first public schools, compared with the earlier schools. A 2001 history of Frederick's Civil War hospital sites, *One Vast Hospital: The Civil War Hospital Sites in Frederick, Maryland after Antietam*, described them because all three schools housed wounded soldiers during the war. Jail Street School was located at 101 W. South Street (the street probably earned that nickname because the jail was located on it). The building was constructed in 1839 and was a primary school until it closed in 1913. Primary School 71, located at 517 and 519 N. Market Street, was constructed before 1844, but only the ground floor of the north building was used as a school. The remaining space was residential. In the mid-1870s, the building housed the female department of Primary School 72, the boys' school across the street at 520 N. Market Street. The building was divided and sold in 1877. Primary School 72 was constructed in the 1840s, after Trustees for the Board of Education bought it in 1841. By the 1870s, the building's name changed to Primary School 9. In 1895, it was demolished and replaced with a six-room brick school that became the new location of the Boys High School, which was begun in 1891 at another location.

Two more churches began to serve the growing community of Frederick, particularly blacks. Quinn Chapel African Methodist Episcopal Church had its roots in meetings of free blacks that began in approximately 1800 because they were not welcome in white churches. The congregation lived along East, Maxwell, Fourth, and Fifth Streets. Calling themselves the Bethel congregation, they met at a wooden lumber shop on the 100 block of East Third Street. In 1819, this congregation bought the machine shop next door. Reverend David Smith led services as part of his circuit, which encompassed Maryland and Pennsylvania. In 1835, the congregation changed its name to Quinn African Methodist Episcopal. Its first brick church was consecrated in 1839. In the records of the 1845 A.M.E. conference in Baltimore, Quinn is listed as having a Sabbath school with two teachers and 25 scholars. The basement of this church also was a stop on the Underground Railroad. The second floor of the church was built in 1855.

On the south side of town, Asbury Methodist Episcopal Church was a diverse congregation that welcomed not only free and enslaved blacks, but also whites. The church began in 1811, when William Hammond, a free black man, paid $64 for a lot on East All Saints Street next to the original All Saints Episcopal Church. Hammond conveyed the lot to Asbury trustees, and the church was constructed in 1818. It also was known as the "Old Hill Church." The building was enlarged in 1850, and was incorporated in 1870 as Asbury Methodist Episcopal Church. It was not until 1921 that the church relocated to its present site at West All Saints Street and South Court Street, after buying the lot in 1912.

Frederick in the New Nation

As the existence of these churches shows, although severely restricted, Frederick's black residents were able to work around some of the restrictions and form their own communities. The number of free blacks in Frederick County increased dramatically between 1790 and 1820, from 213 to 1,777. Their numbers grew even more in 1830 and 1840, to 2,716 and then to 2,985. Many of these people probably migrated to Frederick. Severe racism enforced by laws and other restrictions made life difficult and dangerous. Whites worried about the increase in freed blacks, partly because blacks competed with whites for jobs in trades, as tutors, and as nannies for white children. Maryland passed a law in 1807 preventing the entry into the state of free blacks and "mulattos," a term that referred to people of black and white parentage. In June 1817, a local law forbade slaves from being out after 10 p.m. Those who broke the curfew faced arrest, jail, and up to 39 lashes. This curfew also applied to freed people. Freed blacks also faced the danger of being sold into slavery. Frederick authorized the sheriff to capture black people under suspicion of being fugitive slaves, and a representative of the South's largest slave-trading firm, Franklin and Armfield, had an office in Frederick at Union Tavern.

"Being free was not really free because you had certain places and certain lines you had to walk," writer and historian Kathleen Snowden said in the 1997 documentary *Up from the Meadows*, a history of African Americans in Frederick County.

Still, free blacks formed communities. Some people amassed enough money to buy family members out of slavery. Charles Fortune, a free black man in Frederick, bought his wife, Phoebe, for £30. William Tillman, who owned real estate in Frederick, bought his wife and children out of slavery in 1814. These family members retained their "slave" status and were never manumitted, as a form of protection. Free blacks risked being sold into slavery, but people already enslaved did not, even if their owner was another black person. As early as 1825, 20 free blacks owned homes in Frederick, eight on All Saints Street. Most other people lived in rented houses. African-American communities were located on All Saints, South, Fifth, and East Streets. East Street's black community was named "Shab Row," possibly named after an island off the coast of Africa. A few small businesses were begun, such as the eatery and laundry on South Bentz Street begun by William and Ann Smothers. Some Frederick slaves went to the African country Liberia after a local chapter of the Maryland Colonization Society was formed in 1831.

In the 1830s, Frederick once again reaped the benefits of advancements in transportation. The location of a Baltimore and Ohio Railroad station in Frederick reaffirmed the town's status as a local and national crossroads.

Frederick was not a stop on the B&O Railroad's main line. The Frederick-area stop was located about 2 miles south of Frederick, at a valley grade in which the track could be extended more easily than it could into Frederick, and was called Frederick Junction. A branch line was extended to Frederick, and a depot was opened on Carroll Street on December 1, 1831. By 1852, the railroad line reached the Ohio River. The two-story depot in Frederick was 100 feet by 70 feet. When it was demolished in 1911, it was believed to have been the oldest freight depot in the United States. A ticket and passenger office was opened on the southeast corner of All Saints and Market Streets in 1854. The building was furnished with a ticket office, men's and women's parlors, wash rooms, and baggage rooms. The station stopped serving rail passengers on the Baltimore line in 1937, and on the Washington, D.C. line in 1948 (service to Washington began in 1873). Passenger service to Washington moved to South Carroll Street for a year and then was discontinued altogether in 1949. Today the original passenger station serves as a community center.

The train stop made Frederick accessible to several famous visitors. During an 1824 visit to the United States, the French General Marquis de Lafayette came to Frederick on December 24 at the invitation of a local committee. Many local men had served under Lafayette's command during the Revolutionary War. Lafayette was greeted at the Monocacy River bridge and given a military escort into town in an elaborate carriage. The procession traveled to South Market Street, where a temporary arch was erected in his honor, and then to the courthouse where a speech was delivered by William Ross, Esq. Lafayette was honored at an elaborate dinner at Talbott's Tavern. The next day at Talbott's, he received any Frederick citizen interested in talking with him, and later attended a ball in his honor. He remained in Frederick until December 31.

Andrew Jackson traveled through Frederick in May 1824 as a general, and at the beginning and end of his two terms as president of the United States. Traveling from his Tennessee home, the Hermitage, to Washington for his inauguration in 1829, Jackson stayed overnight at Talbott's City Hotel. According to the *Frederick Town Herald*, cannon fire and the ringing of bells announced his arrival. Jackson passed through again in 1837, on his way back to Tennessee after serving his two terms as President.

Two other presidents visited Frederick during this period. Recently elected President Martin Van Buren stopped at Robert's Tavern in 1837, and President-elect William Henry Harrison arrived by stage in Frederick on February 5, 1841. The stopover might have contributed to his death a few short months into his presidency. Harrison ate dinner at Dorsey's City Hotel, where a large crowd met him. After dinner, he spoke briefly to the crowd, thanking them for helping nominate him, but said he was very tired. Harrison walked to the B&O train depot and boarded the 10 p.m. train to Baltimore. The campaign and the journey to Washington wore down the 68-year-old, and some believed he died from the effects of a cold he caught in Frederick.

Frederick residents were civically active during this period. Many read the newspapers that sprouted after the Revolution, several of which were strongly political and partisan. The *Frederick Town Herald* began in 1802 and was closed down in 1861 by military authorities because its publisher was a supporter of the South. An earlier publisher of the periodical was John P. Thompson, a Federalist who opposed Thomas Jefferson. Jefferson supporter John B. Colvin published the *Republican Advocate* from 1803 to 1811. He also owned another newspaper in town, the *Independent American Volunteer*, run by William B. Underwood. Charles T. Melsheimer published *The Plain Dealer* from 1812 to 1815. The *Chronicle* appeared in 1818, and the religious paper *The Family Gazette* was published in 1820. Other papers included the *Family Visitor*, a literary paper; the *Lutheran Evangelical Intelligencer*; the *Reservoir and Public Reflector*, which advocated a waterworks; the humorous paper the *Intellectual Regale and Evening Companion*; and *The People*. Six more newspapers were founded in the 1830s and the 1840s.

Another source of information about daily life in nineteenth-century Frederick is the diary of West Patrick Street resident Jacob Engelbrecht, whose observations spanned 60 years, from 1819 to his death in 1878. The first-generation German American recorded a variety of news and observations of local, regional, and national importance, from Presidential elections to the local weather. His pithy and precise observations provide a thorough record of local news such as births, deaths, court cases, and other aspects of everyday life in Frederick. For instance, on July 31, 1820, he wrote that four Osage Indians passed through town from Washington, D.C. the previous day, on their way back to St. Louis, Missouri, after negotiating a land treaty. Earlier that year, on April 2, Easter Sunday, he noted that it snowed that day. "It being the first snowy Easter I ever saw, is the reason I mention it. The fruit trees, such as apricots are in blossom and the peach trees ready to burst with blossom is something very novel and so forth." Later that day, he noted that it snowed all day and the snow was 4 inches deep.

Newspapers described the entertainment available in Frederick. All kinds of theatrical performances, animal exhibitions, and circus acts came to town. In 1802, Mr. Powers the ventriloquist performed at Baer's ball room. Shimmell's tavern hosted an exhibition of an African lion, a buffalo, an elk, and a six-legged calf in 1821. Williams & Herbert's company of tragedians performed at City Hall in 1822. The same year, a company of rope-dancers performed, comprising three Italians, two Spaniards, and one Chinese. In 1826, curiosity-seekers could watch a circus of eight men and 18 horses at the barracks grounds and look at Magee, the "Irish giant." The Prussian singer Carl Blisse performed in 1830, and in 1832 the Siamese twins Chang and Eng came to town. Apparently, entertainment was easy to come by in nineteenth-century Frederick.

Of course, not all was happy. As part of a larger epidemic, cholera struck Frederick in September 1832. The first victims were residents of the almshouse outside Frederick and Irish laborers on the Chesapeake and Ohio Canal who lived in town. The disease killed many people in the next two months. Cholera scares occurred over the next two decades, especially in 1833, 1849, and 1854.

Much more serious matters would intrude within a few years. Nationally, fierce disputes were brewing over slavery, states' rights, and sectionalism. The fate of the nation would be decided in the Civil War, and once again, Frederick would serve as a crossroads and as the stage for events of national significance.

Chapter Four

THE CIVIL WAR (1850–1865)

Life in Frederick proceeded peacefully for a few years until the war of words between North and South escalated into a war of weapons.

According to the 1850 federal census, Frederick's population reached 6,027 and comprised 4,783 whites, 825 free blacks and mulattos, and 419 slaves. Free blacks and mulattos accounted for slightly more than 20 percent of the city's residents. Nearly 12 percent of the city's white population was foreign-born.

Of the 1,331 people whose occupations were noted in census records, 293 were laborers. This category included by far the greatest number of Fredericktonians and was comparable to the figure compiled for the rest of Frederick County. The city also was plentiful in shoemakers, carpenters, merchants, clerks, tailors, and tanners. Other occupations whose members participated in the commerce of Frederick included blacksmiths, butchers, coopers, brickmakers, and stone masons. These occupations corresponded with the prevalence of "small, hand industry" in the larger Frederick County, as described by Mary Fitzhugh Hitselberger and John Philip Dern, who analyzed Frederick County data from the 1850 federal census. Professionals included 31 lawyers, 20 physicians, 11 druggists, and 16 schoolteachers. With stagecoaches and wagons the common form of transportation, eight coachmakers, four wagon makers, and five stage drivers worked in Frederick.

In the 1850 federal slave census, 180 Frederick residents were listed as slaveholders. They included such residents as Hiram Winchester, the founder of the Frederick Female Seminary, and Barbara Fritchie, who would become famous during the Civil War for supposedly defying Confederate General Stonewall Jackson. Individual slaveowners in Frederick held relatively few slaves, compared to large plantation owners in rural Frederick County who needed more labor. The number of slaves owned by individuals in Frederick in 1850 ranged from one to ten. A majority owned fewer than five.

Mount Olivet Cemetery opened in 1852. The new cemetery was developed as part of the transition in Frederick from burials in church yards, as those graveyards filled. Mount Olivet was religiously affiliated; the 1853 map of Frederick labeled it the "Protestant cemetery." St. John's Catholic Cemetery opened on the northwest corner of East and Third Streets in 1845, but a burial was recorded as early as 1832, of a free black man named Henry who died of cholera. The 1853 map also depicted the "colored people's grave yard" at the northwest corner of Fifth Street and Chapel Alley, known as Laboring Sons. This cemetery was established in 1851 by the Beneficial Society of the Laboring Sons of Frederick. The city acquired this property in 1949, and turned it into a playground. The city established a memorial park on the site in July 2003 to

Continued on page 113

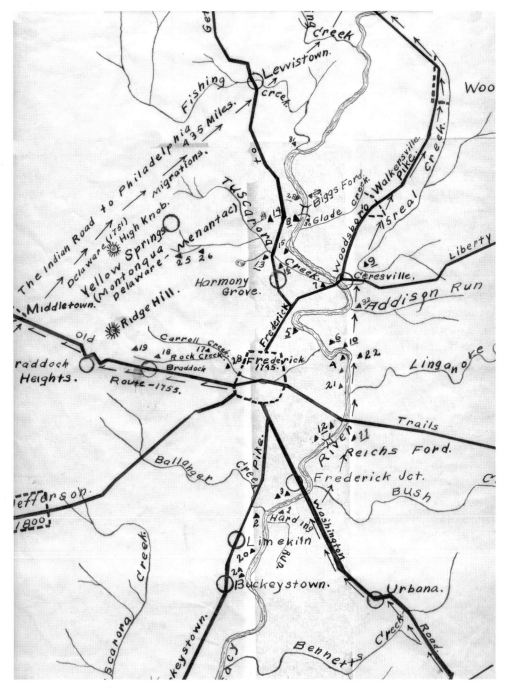

In the 1930s, local amateur archeologist E. Ralston Goldsborough created this map of Native American settlement and occupancy in the Frederick vicinity, titled "Village sites on the Monocacy River." This map resulted from a Works Progress Administration grant he received to study Indian sites in the Monocacy Valley. (Courtesy of the Historical Society of Frederick County.)

Daniel Dulany, also known as Daniel Dulany the Elder, laid out Frederick Town in 1745. (Courtesy of the Historical Society of Frederick County.)

All Saints Episcopal Church moved to this location on West Church Street in 1856. The parish's first church in Frederick was built in 1750 on East All Saints Street. (Courtesy of the Historical Society of Frederick County.)

Frederick Town likely was named for Frederick Calvert, sixth and last Lord Baltimore. (Courtesy of the Historical Society of Frederick County.)

George Washington's headquarters, c. 1908, housed the young aide to British General Edward Braddock before the general's ill-fated march to Fort Duquesne in 1755. The building was located on West All Saints Street until it was torn down in 1913. (Courtesy of the Historical Society of Frederick County.)

The Stamp Act repudiation of 1765 is believed to have been recorded at this home at 103 Record Street. (Courtesy of the Historical Society of Frederick County.)

OLD COURT HOUSE, 1785.

The second, larger Frederick County Courthouse was built in 1785. (Courtesy of the Historical Society of Frederick County.)

FRIENDLY HINTS ON VARIOUS SUBJECT

ORDER AND ECONOMY

Order is Heaven's first law. Says Mr. Pope.

THOUSANDS of the human family are reduced to beggary and wretchedness thro' want of order and regularity in business. Live by rule, and conduct all your business after some fixed plan, which is best calculated to fit your particular calling or possession in life. Rise at an early hour, and refreshing your mind by reading, meditation and prayer, attend with diligence to the business of your calling. From which none, however wealthy, ought to be exempted. For all are in duty bound to make the world richer and better by living in it...

THE DRUNKARD'S LOOKING GLASS.

Here each, who looks may plainly see,
What fools all drunken people be.
Don't break this glass, intemp'rate friend,
But strive your future life to mend.

AGAINST SABBATH BREAKING.

"*Remember the Sabbath day to keep it holy.*"

THESE are not the words of a fellow creature, else we might dispute their authority...

THUS SAITH THE LORD ALMIGHTY.

"*Thou shalt not take my name in vain.*"

EXTRACTS FROM DR. FRANKLIN'S WAY TO WEALTH.

GOD helps them, who help themselves.
Sloth, like rust, consumes faster than labor wears. The key that is used, is always bright.
The sleeping fox catches no poultry; and there will be sleeping enough in the grave.
Lost time is never found again. Sloth makes all things difficult, but industry makes all things easy.
Drive thy business, let not that drive thee. Early to bed and early to rise, makes a man healthy, wealthy and wise.
There are no gains without pains. Many, without labor would live by their wits, but they break for the want of stock. Keep thy shop, and thy shop will keep thee.
The eye of a master will do more work than both his hands.
What maintains one vice, would bring up two children.

THE LORD'S PRAYER, TEN COMMANDMENTS,

AND SOME PIOUS INSTRUCTIONS FROM DR. WATTS AND DR. DODDRIDGE,

CALCULATED TO ENTERTAIN AND IMPROVE THE MINDS OF CHILDREN.

The Lord's Prayer.

Our Father, who art in heaven, hallowed be thy name. Thy kingdom come. Thy will be done on earth, as it is in heaven. Give us this day our daily bread; and forgive us our debts, as we forgive our debtors. And lead us not into temptation, but deliver us from evil. For thine is the kingdom, and the power, and the glory forever. Amen.

QUESTIONS AND ANSWERS.

Q. Who made you? A. God.

THE GOLDEN RULE.

Be ye to others kind and true,
As you'd have others be to you,
And neither do nor say to none,
What e'er you would not take again.

AN EVENING VERSE.

Now I lay me down to sleep,
I pray the Lord my soul to keep;
If I should die before I wake,
I pray the Lord my soul to take.

A MORNING VERSE.

The morning light now peeping...
With gratitude let me arise,
To praise my God for favors given,
And ask his guidance safe to heaven,

PIOUS INSTRUCTIONS.

Children in years and knowledge young,
Your parent's hope, your parent's joy,
Attend the counsels of my tongue,
Let pious thoughts your minds employ.

Mathias Bartgis, a Frederick Town printer, produced "Friendly Hints on Various Subjects" in the 1780s. (Courtesy of the Historical Society of Frederick County.)

Thomas Johnson, the first governor of Maryland, was a Frederick Town resident from the mid-1770s to 1819. (Courtesy of the Historical Society of Frederick County.)

Friedrich Heinrich Scheer commanded two regiments of Hessian prisoners of war held in Frederick Town. (Courtesy of the Historical Society of Frederick County.)

This receipt documents Frederick Town resident James Smith's 1794 purchase of slaves. (Courtesy of the Historical Society of Frederick County.)

HISTORIC OLD STONE TAVERN, FREDERICK, MD.

The Old Stone Tavern at Patrick and Jefferson Streets fed and housed travelers in the early nineteenth century. (Courtesy of the Historical Society of Frederick County.)

Lotts & Houses in Frederick Town Dist.

Owners & poss's Names	N° of Lotts	By whom are paid if any	Ground Rents
Elijah Bratly	1		
John Brunner	1/4		
Andrew Boyd	1		
Christopher Barkman	1/2	Madam De Court for 1/2 Lott £10	
Conrod Baher	1		
Wm. M. Beall	2		
Frederick Bougher	5		
" Ditto	3		
" Ditto	2		
" Ditto	1/2		
Godfrey Brown	1		
Tobias Butler	1/2		
Henry Bautz	2 1/4		
Michael Baltzell	1/2. 8 3/4		
Jacob Bartle	1		
John Buckeus	1/4		
Valentine Brother	6 1/2		
" Ditto	7/12		
George Baer (Mason)	1/2		
Francis Baker	1/4		
Peter Beale	1		
Margaret Brengle	1		
Frederick Baher	1/2	John Sadler £15	
George Barrick	1/2		
Charles Boly	1		
Peter Bruner Jr	1		
Magdalene Bruner	1		
William Beatty	3		
Lawrence Brengle Jew	1/4		
George Brengle	2 1/2	of a small piece in Bentz Town	
Christopher Berkhartt	1		
Alberdeen Bruner	1	Widow of Elias	

This section of a 1798 list of lot owners in Frederick Town shows that Jews were some of the city's early settlers. However, sometimes they were singled out. Note the term "Jew" written after the names Peter Bruner and Lawrence Brengle, located near the bottom of the list. (Courtesy of the Maryland State Archives [MSA C755-2, MDHR 19,268, Location 1/54/10/14].)

The first St. John's Catholic Church was built in 1800, but the current church, pictured here, was built in 1833. (Courtesy of the Historical Society of Frederick County.)

Francis Scott Key, who wrote the "Star-Spangled Banner," was born in Frederick County in 1779 and lived in Frederick Town from 1801 to 1805. (Courtesy of the Historical Society of Frederick County.)

Supreme Court Justice Roger Brooke Taney lived in Frederick Town from 1801 to 1823. (Courtesy of the Historical Society of Frederick County.)

This early twentieth-century postcard displays the "Star-Spangled Banner," which Francis Scott Key wrote in 1814. (Courtesy of the Historical Society of Frederick County.)

These slave quarters were located behind Roger Brooke Taney's house on South Bentz Street. (Courtesy of the Historical Society of Frederick County.)

Roger Brooke Taney might have lived in this house on South Bentz Street with his wife, Anne Key, the sister of Francis Scott Key, and their daughters. (Courtesy of the Historical Society of Frederick County.)

Hiram Winchester came to Frederick in 1830 and began the Frederick Female Seminary in 1830 on North Market Street. He erected two ornate classical buildings on East Church Street and moved the school to them in 1845. (Courtesy of the Historical Society of Frederick County.)

The cannon in the lower left corner of this c. 1904 photo of West Fourth Street was used to celebrate James K. Polk's victory in the 1844 presidential election. The cannon exploded after its gunner, a man named Duvall, filled the barrel with clay. (Courtesy of the Historical Society of Frederick County.)

THIRD AND LAST CONCERT!!!

TICKETS REDUCED TO 25 CENTS!

THE

ORPHEAN FAMILY,

Would respectfully announce to the Ladies and Gentlemen of Frederick, that they will give one more entertainment of

VOCAL MUSIC,

At the MASONIC HALL,

This (Monday) Evening,

On which occasion they will introduce a new programme, and the tickets will be but **25** cents each.

☞Doors open **7 1-2** o'clock. Concert to commence at a **1-4** past 8.

☞The Tickets may be obtained, with programmes at the door.

No postponement on account of weather.

☞POSITIVELY NO HALF PRICE TICKETS.
JUNE 22nd, 1846.

Printed at the Office of the "EXAMINER," Frederick City, Md.

An 1846 advertisement announces a local performance of the Orphean family. (Courtesy of the Historical Society of Frederick County.)

Confederate General Stonewall Jackson wanted to attend worship services at the Presbyterian Church during the Confederate occupation of Frederick in 1862, but services were not available. (Courtesy of the Maryland Room of the C. Burr Artz Library.)

TO THE PEOPLE OF FRED'K. COUNTY.

FELLOW-CITIZENS,

The widespread prevalence of the political heresy of Secession which has resulted in the withdrawal of seven States from that Union which for nearly a century has been our pride and boast, demands our instant action, so that our silence may not be misconstrued and that our example may afford moral aid and encouragement to the loyal & patriotic men who still cling to their Country with unabated love and fidelity.

Notwithstanding the many grievances of which the South justly complains, and against which none has juster cause for remonstrance than the State of Maryland, we hold that *Secession is no remedy* for ...

We hold that in a government of laws, the first ... of every citizen is obedience ... justice or wrong may be perpetrated, in a free government where the largest exercise of liberty compatible with the stability of government and the security of the people is guaranteed to every individual, no such wrong or injustice can be permanent, but that a fair and candid appeal to the honesty and intelligence of the people of the whole country, will inevitably result in a full and cordial recognition of all our constitutional rights and the removal of all our existing grounds of complaint.

We hold that the temporary and accidental triumph of the Republican Party in the election of a President, while the real and substantial power of the government remained in the hands of their opponents, was no such overwhelming calamity as to compel or justify the dissolution of this Confederacy; the total abandonment of our rights and privileges in the Union and the renunciation of the glorious heritage bequeathed to us by our Revolutionary ancestors.

We hold that the remedy for all these things is to be found, not in Secession, but at the ballot-box; and we feel justified in believing that there is already a returning sense of justice on the part of our Northern brethren.

Therefore, the undersigned earnestly invite their fellow-citizens of Frederick County, who stand by the Union of these States and oppose Secession for any past or present cause, to unite with them in

MASS CONVENTION

AT THE COURT HOUSE, IN THE CITY OF FREDERICK AT 10 O'CLOCK, A. M.,
ON TUESDAY, THE 26TH DAY OF MARCH, 1861,

to form a Union Organization in this County and to take steps for holding a Union State Convention at an early day thereafter.

Jacob Bear, R. Potts, L. J. Brengle, John Loats, Chas E Trail, Wm P Maulsby, James Cooper, Frederick Schley, Grayson Eichelberger, James Whitehill, Edward Shriver, Adam Wolfe, Nicholas Whitmore, Wm D Reese, J W L Carty, Basil Norris, W Tyler, Sr, Jacob Markell, R Y Stokes, John Schreiner, R H Macgill, P L Storm, W B Tyler, Francis Markell, P M Englebrecht, George Markell, Lewis Markell, Emanuel Mantz, John Ramsburgh, Jacob Knauff, George A. Abbott, John McPherson, Saml. B. Preston, Dewalt Willard, Samuel Carmack, J. McPherson, Sebast'n Ramsburg, Jacob Grove, Jacob Riehl, John T. Green, Hiram Schmsler, Philip Cramer.

Otho Norris, J D Getzendanner, Ulysses Hobbs, Charles Cole, J A Simmons, Frederick Keefer, Christian Steiner, Charles Lease, James T Smith, D C Winebrenner, James Hopwood, Barney Fisher, James Hergesheimer, Zephaniah Harrison, A Gault, Edward Buckey, Thos H Holbrunner, John Mackchney, Edward Sinn, Val S Brunner, Wm G Cole, Tobias Haller, Jacob Stimmel, John J Woodward, L M Schaeffer, Wm G Schaeffer, M Keefer, T J McGill, George Salmon, Jonathan T. Wilson, William H. James, Wm. B. Tabler, Wm. T. Gittings, Isaac Keller, Wm. T. Preston, W James Williamson, Wm. M. Derr, John M. Ebert, William H. Grove, David K. Schaeffer, Charles H Keefer, George W Cramer.

Jacob Sahm, Jacob Reifsnider, Charles E Mealey, Charles W Haller, Frederick Mala, Geo C Johnson, Charles Mantz, E Y Goldsborough, Samuel R Hogg, Jacob Fox, David Weaver, Wm Johnston, Edward Trail, W G Moran, Daniel Haller, George Engelbrecht, Thomas M Markell, William T Haller, John E Sifford, John Goldsborough, George F Webster, G W Delaplane, Daniel Sweeney, E Albaugh, George W. Ulrich, Abraham Haff, Charles E Albaugh, D T Ronner, Andrew Boyd, Hiram H. Mullen, John H. Abbott, W. Lechner, R. G. McPherson, William Stokes, B. Cunningham, John H. Keller, James M. Harding, Henry M. Nixdorf, Henry B. Fessler, Samuel B. Ebert, Chas E. Campbell, Philip H Sinn.

Ephraim Creager, Spencer C Jones, Grafton W Elliott, John Poole, Frederick Kehler, Jacob Detre, Wilson R Boyd, Erasmus West, L V Scholl, G R Kephart, Daniel H Rohr, George K Birely, D W Brooks, John Lyeth, I W Suman, John T Schley, Isaiah Mealey, John Sanner, George S Groshon, John B Mumford, Robert Boone, Levi Vanfossen, Dennis Scholl, William H. Brish, Isacher Himbury, William Higgins, Richard T. Dixon, Lewis H. Dill, John J. Suman, Grafton Foot, George Metzger, Adam Custard, G. W. Derizbaugh, T. E. Getzendanner, Benjamin Ebert, G. P. Ramsburg, H. F. Schmoller, Samuel Haller, George W Custard, N. H. Pitts.

Lewis H. Bennet, P. Jefferson Hawman, Lloyd Dorsey, Robert Shafer, George W. Summers, Henry C. Steiner, John J. Kantner, Lawrence Beatz, Daniel A. Staley, Anthony Kimmel, Francis T. Rhodes, George W. Derr, Isaac P. Suman, George W. L. Bartgis, John Wilson, George Gittinger, James Bruner, H. K. Hilton, Michael Englebrecht, William Glessner, George Kantner, A. B. Hunt, ..., W. R. Sanderson, W. J. Lynn Smith, Simon Parsons, Frederick Shipley, Abraham Kemp, George M. Tyler, Maurice Albaugh, William T. Duvall, Charles H. Eader, Jacob Leitich, Michael H. Haller, John Stimmel, Charles W. Miller, Benjamin Routzahn, George D. Miller, A. P. Kessler, William H. Rice, Henry A. Cole.

Daniel S. Loy, William Dean, W. H. C. Dean, Josiah Harrison, Harrison Conley, Nicholas T. Haller, L. M. Englebrecht, James W. Phebus, C Getzendanner, John T. Martin, Henry Lorentz, William Lorentz, John Routzahn, Mathias Ahalt, John Sifford, Geo T. Willard, Thomas Hooper, John Cramer, James W. Hood, J George Sinn, J. R. Marken, John Hooper, James Hooper, W. B. R. Kelly, O. F. Butler, Gideon Bantz, David Kenega, Upton Buhrman, W. L. Hays, A. E. Smith, Clark Eldridge, M. G. Arnold, Hanson T. C. Green, J. J. Moenn, George R. Dennis, Dr. J. Bonne, L. A. Brengle, Jr., G. J. Dull, Isaac Wisong, T. M. Morgan, jr.

Printed at the Office of "The Maryland Union" Frederick, Md. [March 19, 1861.

Confederate General Robert E. Lee issued this proclamation to entice Maryland residents to join the Confederate cause. (Courtesy of the Historical Society of Frederick County.)

PROCLAMATION OF GENERAL LEE.

HEADQUARTERS ARMY N. VA. }
Near Fredericktown, Sept. 8, 1862. }

TO THE PEOPLE OF MARYLAND:

It is right that you should know the purpose that has brought the Army under my command within the limits of your State, so far as that purpose concerns yourselves.

The People of the Confederate States have long watched, with the deepest sympathy, the wrongs and outrages that have been inflicted upon the Citizens of a Commonwealth, allied to the States of the South by the strongest social, political and commercial ties. They have seen with profound indignation their sister States deprived of every right, and reduced to the condition of a conquered province.

Under the pretense of supporting the constitution, but in violation of its most valuable provisions, your Citizens have been arrested and imprisoned upon no charge, and contrary to all forms of law; the faithful and manly protest against this outrage made by the venerable and illustrious Marylander to whom in better days no citizen appealed for right in vain, was treated with scorn and contempt; the government of your chief city has been usurped by armed strangers; your Legislature has been dissolved by the unlawful arrest of its members; freedom of the press and of speech has been suppressed; words have been declared offences by an arbitrary decree of the Federal Executive, and citizens ordered to be tried by a military commission for what they may dare to speak.

Believing that the people of Maryland possessed a spirit too lofty to submit to such a government, the people of the South have long wished to aid you in throwing off this foreign yoke to enable you again to enjoy the inalienable rights of freemen, and restore independence and sovereignty to your State. In obedience to this wish, our army has come among you, and is prepared to assist you with the power of its arms in regaining the rights of which you have been despoiled. This, Citizens of Maryland, is our mission, so far as you are concerned. No restraint upon your free will is intended, no intimidation will be allowed. Within the limits of this army, at least, Marylanders shall once more enjoy their ancient freedom of thought and speech. We know no enemies among you, and will protect all of every opinion. It is for you to decide your destiny, freely and without constraint. This Army will respect your choice, whatever it may be; and while the Southern people will rejoice to welcome you to your natural position among them, they will only welcome you when you come of your own free will.

R. E. LEE, General Commanding.

Confederate troops marched west on East Patrick Street in 1862. (Courtesy of the Historical Society of Frederick County.)

Barbara Fritchie
at the age of 92.

Barbara Fritchie, the subject of John Greenleaf Whittier's famous poem, moved to her West Patrick Street home on the banks of Carroll Creek in the late 1700s. (Courtesy of the Historical Society of Frederick County.)

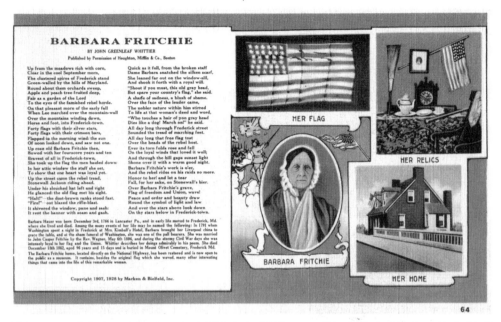

This postcard depicts John Greenleaf Whittier's 1863 poem "The Ballad of Barbara Freitchie," which immortalized the Frederick resident but is widely believed to be more legend than reality. (Courtesy of the Historical Society of Frederick County.)

Frederick received this receipt for payment of a $200,000 ransom to Confederate General Jubal Early in 1864. (Courtesy of the Historical Society of Frederick County.)

This drawing in Harper's Weekly *depicts President Abraham Lincoln's arrival at the B&O Railroad station in Frederick in October 1862, en route to his visits of the battlefields of Antietam and South Mountain. (Courtesy of the Historical Society of Frederick County.)*

NOTICE!

With feelings of deep regret, I have to announce to the citizens of Frederick, the melancholy intelligence of the assination of President LINCOLN, on Friday night, the 14th instant, and therefore respectfully request that the business places in this city, be closed from 12 o'clock, M., TO-DAY, and that appropriate public services be held in the different Churches at 4 o'clock, P. M., as a mark of respect for the deceased.

J. ENGELBRECHT,
Mayor.

Mayor's Office, April 15th, 1865.

Mayor Jacob Engelbrecht used this public notice to inform Frederick residents of President Lincoln's assassination in April 1865. (Courtesy of the Historical Society of Frederick County.)

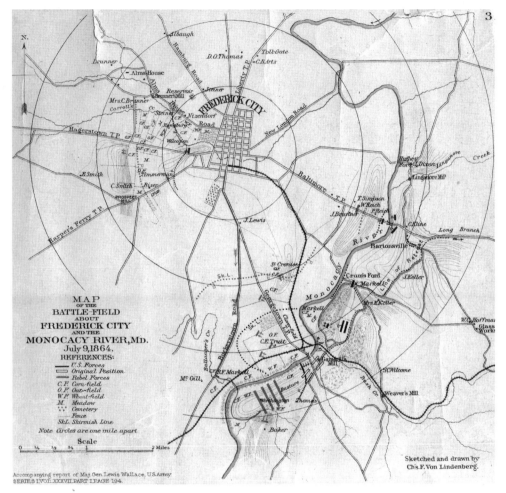

This map depicts battlefield sites south of Frederick in 1864 during the Battle of the Monocacy. (Courtesy of the Historical Society of Frederick County.)

Supporters of Republican Presidential candidate Benjamin Harrison gathered for a political rally at the northeast corner of Church and Court Streets in 1888. (Courtesy of the Historical Society of Frederick County.)

West Patrick Street, facing west, suffered in the devastating 1868 flood of Carroll Creek. (Courtesy of the Historical Society of Frederick County.)

John D. Hendrickson's Dry Goods Store was located on North Market Street in 1890. (Courtesy of the Historical Society of Frederick County.)

The J. Tyson and Son fertilizer manufacturing firm was located on South Carroll Street in 1895. (Courtesy of the Historical Society of Frederick County.)

The Park Hotel at West Church and Court Streets, 1896, was one of several hotels in town. (Courtesy of the Historical Society of Frederick County.)

Students at Maryland School for the Deaf learn pronunciation from their teacher in 1890. (Courtesy of the Historical Society of Frederick County.)

Girls at Loats orphanage lived in a large house at 24 E. Church Street. Today the building houses the Historical Society of Frederick County. (Courtesy of the Historical Society of Frederick County.)

EAST HALL.

COLLEGE BUILDINGS.

WEST HALL.

Winchester Hall housed the Woman's College when this photo was taken in 1900. (Courtesy of the Historical Society of Frederick County.)

The West Seventh Street reservoir was under construction in the late 1890s. The reservoir was located at the site of Max Kehne Park. (Courtesy of the Historical Society of Frederick County.)

The fountain at North Market and Seventh Streets, shown here in 1900, is still operating today, although the corner is much busier. (Courtesy of the Historical Society of Frederick County.)

The Young Men's Christian Association building on the southeast corner of Church and Court Streets was built in 1907 and demolished in the mid-1960s. (Courtesy of the Historical Society of Frederick County.)

The Emergency Hospital was opened in 1903 at 135 S. Market Street by Frederick County doctors who did not want the new Frederick City Hospital to be managed by the non-professional Frederick City Hospital Association, a group of prominent local women. The dispute was resolved in 1906. (Courtesy of the Historical Society of Frederick County.)

United Fire Company 3 on South Market Street, shown here in 1910, has operated this station since 1845. (Courtesy of the Historical Society of Frederick County.)

Frederick City Hospital, bordered by Seventh Street, Park Place, and Park Avenue, opened in 1902 and is shown here in 1908. (Courtesy of the Historical Society of Frederick County.)

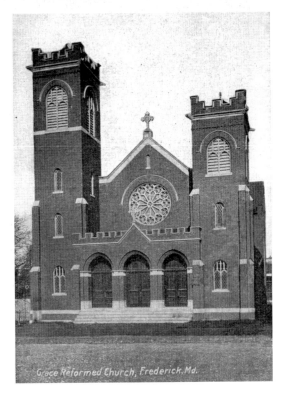

Grace Reformed Church on East Second Street, shown in 1913, formed in 1898 and built the church in 1903. (Courtesy of the Historical Society of Frederick County.)

This 1913 postcard depicts the Baltimore & Ohio Railroad station at the southeast corner of East All Saints and Market Streets. (Courtesy of the Maryland Room of the C. Burr Artz Library.)

An early twentieth century postcard depicts Clarke Place, located in southern Frederick east of South Market Street. (Courtesy of the Maryland Room of the C. Burr Artz Library.)

The Opera House was located in the 100 block of North Market Street. The Opera House hosted operas, dramas, and other live performances, and later showed movies. (Courtesy of the Historical Society of Frederick County.)

The Hood College fielded a basketball team, shown here in 1918. (Courtesy of the Historical Society of Frederick County.)

This photo of Mont Riant, the home of Mr. and Mrs. John E. Price and family, on East Street between Eighth and Ninth Streets, shows how rural East Street still was in the early twentieth century. (Courtesy of the Historical Society of Frederick County.)

Trinity Chapel dominates this 1910 view of West Church Street. (Courtesy of the Historical Society of Frederick County.)

6 p.m.

Hundreds of Frederick residents eyed the skies on August 21, 1911, to watch the first airplane landing in Frederick. Piloted by Lieutenant Hap Arnold and co-pilot Chandler, the plane took off from the Army Aviation School in College Park and landed at Camp Ordway, the present site of Fort Detrick. At the time it was the longest airplane flight. (Courtesy of the Historical Society of Frederick County.)

Girls High School was still located on East Church Street in 1912. (Courtesy of the Historical Society of Frederick County.)

The Boys High School Class of 1913 poses in uniform in front of its building on Elm Street. (Courtesy of the Historical Society of Frederick County.)

Phil's Fruit Store was located on the northwest corner of All Saints and Market Streets, in the early 1900s. (Courtesy of the Maryland Room of the C. Burr Artz Library.)

WASHINGTON STREET SCHOOL, FREDERICK, MD.

Washington Street School, shown in a 1914 postcard, served students in southern Frederick. (Courtesy of the Historical Society of Frederick County.)

Some elements of this c. 1909 photo of Market Street facing south at Church Street are present today. A faded version of the painted sign advertising Rosenour's men's clothing store still graces the side of the Rosenour Building at 37 N. Market Street. (Courtesy of the Historical Society of Frederick County.)

First Baptist Church on West Dill Avenue, shown in 1913, was built in 1905. The present structure was built in 1922. (Courtesy of the Historical Society of Frederick County.)

Methodist Episcopal Church, Frederick, Md.

Methodist Episcopal Church on East Church Street, shown in 1913, was the congregation's third on the site. The congregation had owned the site since 1841. The congregation changed its name to Calvary Methodist Episcopal Church in 1923 and built a larger church and school on the northeast corner of West Second and Bentz Streets in 1930. The City of Frederick eventually purchased the former site and built a parking garage. (Courtesy of the Historical Society of Frederick County.)

Citizens National Bank Building, Frederick, Md.

Citizens National Bank, at the southeast corner of Market and Patrick Streets in 1913, was organized in 1886 by Joseph Dill Baker. (Courtesy of the Historical Society of Frederick County.)

The Frederick Railroad Co. office was located at East Patrick and Carroll Streets c. *1910, when this photo was taken, but today it houses the offices of the* Frederick News-Post *newspaper. (Courtesy of the Historical Society of Frederick County.)*

Montevue Hospital, located west of Rosemont Avenue, in 1914, was built in 1870 to care for the sick, insane, indigent, and poor. (Courtesy of the Historical Society of Frederick County.)

Record Street, shown here in 1922, was part of Daniel Dulany's original layout of Frederick Town. (Courtesy of the Historical Society of Frederick County.)

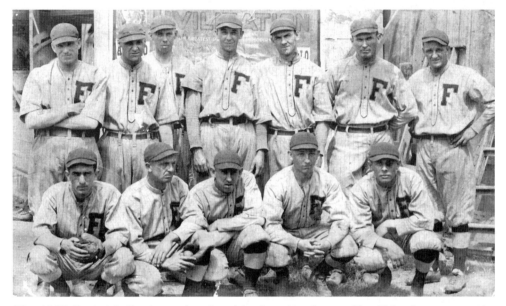

The 1917 Frederick Hustlers, who played in the minor league Blue Ridge League, are the following, from left to right: (front row) Bill Phoenix, shortstop; John Doherty, second base; Monk Walter, outfield; Clyde Barnhart, outfield; Ralph "Monk" Frazier, catcher; (back row) Wick Winslow, pitcher; Bill Mortimer, infield; Bill King, pitcher; Eddie Hook, pitcher; Jake Zinnell, outfield; Tom Crooke, manager/first base; Charlie Maurer, third base. (Courtesy of Shirley Perez of Waynesboro, Pennsylvania, via Mark Zeigler www.blueridgeleague.org.)

Francis Scott Key Hotel on West Patrick Street opened in 1923. (Courtesy of the Maryland Room of the C. Burr Artz Library.)

The Frederick High School Class of 1928 graduated from the school when it was located on Elm Street. (Courtesy of the Historical Society of Frederick County.)

"LILY OF THE SWAMP"

The United Fire Co. pump, known as "Lily of the Swamp," was donated to the Smithsonian Institution shortly after this 1935 photo. (Courtesy of the Maryland Room of the C. Burr Artz Library.)

This 1937 photo depicts the exterior of C. Burr Artz Library at Record and Council Streets. (Courtesy of the Historical Society of Frederick County.)

The Barbara Fritchie Cabins, 230 W. Patrick Street, served vacationers traveling along U.S. Route 40, which was included in the new federal highway system in 1926. (Courtesy of the Maryland Room of the C. Burr Artz Library.)

A crane prepares to move the jug bridge monument, which stood at the Monocacy River bridge from 1808 to 1942, when the bridge collapsed. The monument was moved to East Patrick Street and Bowman Farm Road. (Courtesy of the Historical Society of Frederick County.)

Trolleys traveled down East Patrick Street at Middle Alley in the 1930s. (Courtesy of the Historical Society of Frederick County.)

The Francis Scott Key Hotel marquee was the focal point of the view of West Patrick Street at Market Street in the 1930s. (Courtesy of the Historical Society of Frederick County.)

Trolley tracks extended south on Market Street from Patrick Street in the 1930s. (Courtesy of the Historical Society of Frederick County.)

The Monocacy River bridge east of Frederick collapsed in 1942. (Courtesy of the Historical Society of Frederick County.)

Frederick High School from Culler Lake, Frederick, Maryland — K-71-D-1

Frederick High School, opened in 1940, was photographed from Culler Lake in Baker Park. (Courtesy of the Historical Society of Frederick County.)

This was the interior of Brish Brothers Bazaar, a variety store at 206 W. Patrick Street, in 1940. (Courtesy of the Historical Society of Frederick County.)

This 1955 bird's-eye view depicts Hood College. (Courtesy of the Historical Society of Frederick County.)

Alumnae Hall, Hood College, Frederick, Maryland — K-71-D-5

When it was built in 1914, Alumnae Hall was the first building constructed on the relocated campus of Hood College. (Courtesy of the Historical Society of Frederick County.)

A freight train on East Patrick Street between Carroll and East Streets travels the Hagerstown & Frederick Railway line, in 1948. (Courtesy of the Maryland Room of the C. Burr Artz Library.)

The Hotel Frederick was located at 327 N. Market Street in 1952. (Courtesy of the Historical Society of Frederick County.)

Calvary Methodist Church at Second and Bentz Streets, here in 1952, was constructed in 1930. (Courtesy of the Historical Society of Frederick County.)

Before its development, this section of West Route 40 just outside Frederick was Hillcrest Orchard, owned by E. Dwight McCain. The apple orchard operated in the early and middle twentieth century in what is now western Frederick, on the hilly area on the south side of the present-day Golden Mile retail corridor. (Courtesy of the Historical Society of Frederick County.)

The swimming pool at Baker Park, shown in 1952, was built in 1948. (Courtesy of the Historical Society of Frederick County.)

A trolley on the Hagerstown & Frederick Railway line travels east on West Fifth Street in 1954. (Courtesy of the Maryland Room of the C. Burr Artz Library.)

The Blue Ridge Transportation Co. bus terminal on West Patrick Street, in 1955, was located just west of the Tivoli Theater. (Courtesy of the Maryland Room of the C. Burr Artz Library.)

Former President Harry Truman and former First Lady Bess Truman stopped at Carroll H. Kehne's Gulf service station on West Patrick and Jefferson Streets to buy gas on June 21, 1953. They were driving to Washington, D.C. from Independence, Missouri. (Courtesy of the Historical Society of Frederick County.)

Hagerstown & Frederick Railway Engine 12 traveled on East Street between Second and Third Streets in 1955. (Courtesy of the Maryland Room of the C. Burr Artz Library.)

The foundation of a new building was laid at Frederick High School in 1956, probably the vocational agriculture building. (Courtesy of the Historical Society of Frederick County.)

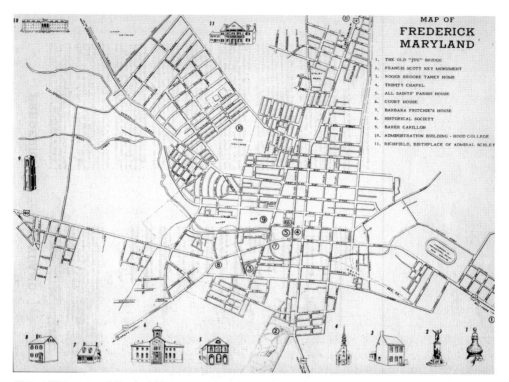

This 1960 map of Frederick shows that Frederick had expanded substantially compared to earlier maps. (Courtesy of the Historical Society of Frederick County.)

East South Street appeared to be residential in 1964. (Courtesy of the Historical Society of Frederick County.)

Marshall Etchison stands on the front step of his music studio, now the Historical Society of Frederick County's Marshall Etchison Bookstore. Etchison's heirs donated many of his antiques and his historical book collection to the Historical Society. (Courtesy of the Historical Society of Frederick County.)

By the time this photo was taken in 1975, Winchester Hall housed the Frederick County government. (Courtesy of the Historical Society of Frederick County.)

West Patrick Street at Jefferson Street was clear for traffic on this sunny winter day in 1964. (Courtesy of the Historical Society of Frederick County.)

The top of the Frederick County Courthouse peeks through the trees in this 1964 view of West Church Street at the Courthouse Square. (Courtesy of the Historical Society of Frederick County.)

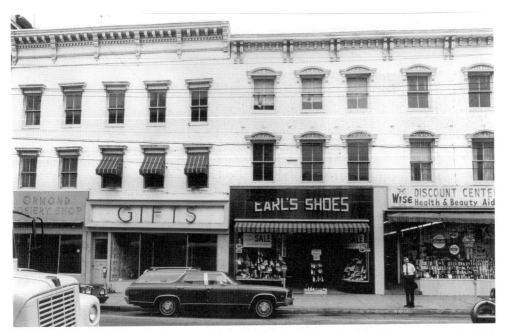

Earl's Shoes was located at 9 N. Market Street and Wise Discount Center occupied 11 N. Market Street in 1972. (Courtesy of the Historical Society of Frederick County.)

Frederick County National Bank occupied the northwest corner of Patrick and Market Streets in this c. 1970 photo. Routzahn and Sons department store is located on the right side of the photo, on the northeast corner. (Courtesy of the Historical Society of Frederick County.)

City Hall, located in the 1862 Frederick County Courthouse, was depicted in this 1990 painting. (Courtesy of the Maryland Room of the C. Burr Artz Library.)

A demonstration Maryland Rail Commuter (MARC) train traveled to Frederick in 1992, nine years before service began. (Courtesy of the Maryland Room of the C. Burr Artz Library.)

The Clustered Spires still dominate the skyline of present-day Frederick. (Courtesy of the Historical Society of Frederick County.)

The Civil War

Continued from page 48

commemorate the former cemetery. Another "colored people's grave yard" was located on the north side of East All Saints Street, the location of Asbury Methodist Episcopal church until 1921. Church yard cemeteries included one at the rear of the Lutheran church on East Church Street, the oldest in Frederick, as well as at All Saints, German Reformed, Methodist, and Presbyterian churches. The German Reformed church also maintained a cemetery at Second and Bentz Streets, replaced by Memorial Park.

The Agricultural Society held an exhibition October 12 to 14, 1853 at the former barracks on South Market Street. The Society was known as the Farmer's Club when it was founded in 1849. The first agricultural exhibition in Frederick County was a cattle show and fair in 1822 at the Monocacy River bridge. The exhibition's sponsor, the Frederick County Agricultural Society, was short-lived. The fairs sponsored by The Agricultural Society continued annually through 1860. The fairs were interrupted by the Civil War, and resumed in 1867. That year, the organization bought 30 acres from General Edward Shriver for a permanent site and established what is known today as the location of the Great Frederick Fair.

By the end of the 1850s, the nation's sectional disagreements came to a head. The conflict exploded on Frederick County's doorstep in 1859, when militant abolitionist John Brown raided the Federal Arsenal at Harper's Ferry, Virginia, located just over the Potomac River from Frederick County. In the dark of night on Sunday, October 16, Brown and a group of 18 men armed with rifles and revolvers took the arsenal's night watchman prisoner. They captured and held several townspeople as hostages and cut telegraph wires to prevent communication. Harassment by armed citizens and Virginia militia members forced Brown and his group to take refuge in an engine house on the arsenal grounds. The group's action was part of a larger movement, led by Brown, to forcibly end slavery and create a new country in the Appalachian mountains for freed slaves. Brown anticipated support from a grassroots coalition of slaves and liberal whites.

Word of the insurrection was carried to Frederick on Monday morning by way of a train that Brown allowed to leave Harper's Ferry. The first reports were wildly exaggerated and suggested that either government employees or local blacks were responsible for the uprising, numbered in the hundreds, and were heavily armed. Three military companies from Frederick offered their services and, authorized by President James Buchanan, headed south to the besieged town that Monday on a train provided by the B&O Railroad. While the Frederick militia guarded the perimeter of the armory, Brown attempted to negotiate with one of the militia commanders, J.T. Sinn, and Colonel Edward Shriver, the leader of the Frederick militia, but failed to secure his release. The insurrection ended 36 hours later when U.S. Marines led by Army Colonel Robert E. Lee and Lieutenant J.E.B. Stuart battered down the engine house door. Brown's men were killed or captured. The Frederick militia returned home on Tuesday, but their work was not complete. Sinn testified at Brown's trial, and Sinn's company defended the jail at Charlestown, where Brown was held, to guard against attempts by abolitionists to free him. Brown was executed for treason in December.

Tensions continued to escalate in 1860. The number of free blacks in Frederick, 1,254, far outnumbered the 443 slaves in the city, but no more manumissions were allowed in

FREDERICK

Maryland after June 1. In Frederick, the year was filled with rallies sponsored by opposing points of view, secession and preservation of the Union, that featured parades and long speeches. Presidential candidate Stephen Douglas spoke at the courthouse on September 7. On December 15, Frederick County residents who supported maintaining the Union met at the courthouse and passed resolutions opposing secession. They called for a county convention to discuss the subject. At the convention two days later, as a sign of the sharp divisions in Frederick County, residents were so closely divided on the issue that a voice vote was impossible. The participants assembled in the courthouse yard to vote. Those favoring the union walked through the east gate, and the secessionists walked through the south gate. The Union supporters won, 314 to 117. Unionists participated in "Liberty pole raisings," in which the United States flag was raised on poles. Flags also were flown from windows and storefronts. Meanwhile, secessionists occupied the Keystone Club building in Frederick. On December 20, 1860, the first of the secessionist-minded states put words into action, when South Carolina seceded from the Union. By February, six other states had seceded. These seven states wrote a constitution for the Confederate States of America and named Jefferson Davis president. Frederick County supporters of the Union made a last-ditch attempt to prevent war by calling for a mass convention on March 26. The Civil War began on April 12, 1861, when the Confederates bombarded Fort Sumter, South Carolina. The announcement drew news-hungry crowds to the office of the *Examiner* newspaper.

War alarmed Maryland citizens and state officials, many of whom who had southern sympathies and allowed slavery in their state but did not want to disrupt the Union. They also knew that Maryland's geographic position as a border state close to the nation's capital would make the state a battleground. Residents of the city of Frederick knew they and greater Frederick County were vulnerable. As they had several times previously, Frederick residents prepared for a war that would tax their resources, divide their loyalties, and disrupt their lives. The rallies and speeches of the previous months revealed the divided loyalties of Frederick citizens, but those loyalties were not easily held when it meant disagreeing with neighbors, friends, and family. "It was a trying time; a time when friends and neighbors were compelled to look into each other's faces with feelings of doubt and apprehension," according to *History of Western Maryland*. "Estrangements began in circles that had been closely knit together for years in the quiet activities of a complacent life in a well-ordered community."

Two weeks after Fort Sumter, on April 26, the Maryland General Assembly convened in Frederick because federal troops had surrounded Annapolis, the state capital. President Lincoln ordered federal troops to Maryland because he feared that secessionists would capture Washington, D.C. by moving through Maryland from Baltimore, the Eastern Shore, or Virginia. In Frederick, the legislature met in Kemp Hall, a building located on the southeast corner of Market and Church Streets that was owned by the Reformed Church. The Senate met on the second floor and the House of Delegates convened on the third floor. Governor Hicks stayed at the Dill House on West Church Street during the sessions to ensure that the legislature did not exceed its constitutional authority. Frederick residents were hospitable, even to Assembly members with whom they disagreed. But the legislature's presence was disruptive. According to newspaper accounts, Frederick was under nightly guard, and the guards had to contend with drunken Assembly members who stayed out late and got lost. On May 8, the county courthouse burned, and secessionists and Union supporters accused each other of arson. A new courthouse was constructed in 1862. Frederick municipal government uses the building today.

The legislature's session lasted until May 14, and the Assembly reconvened on June 4. During this second session, the legislature directed Governor Thomas Holliday Hicks to return all arms issued to militias throughout the state. The Frederick Home Guard and most other militias refused—the Frederick Home Guard pledged to fight the order "at all hazards and unto death"—and the legislature rescinded its order.

But the most significant and dramatic event associated with the General Assembly's Frederick sessions occurred in a session that began on September 17. Letters had been intercepted that implied that secessionist legislators, who dominated the Assembly, were in league with Confederates in Virginia to occupy Frederick and force the passage of a law committing Maryland to secede. By the date the session began, Maryland was under federal control, and the U.S. secretary of war ordered the arrest of all secessionist legislators and officers of the legislature. When the legislature reconvened September 17, not enough legislators were present to form a quorum, so a secession resolution could not be passed. The city had been surrounded, and most of the legislators and several officers were arrested. Thus, a declaration of secession was prevented.

Meanwhile, troops moved into and out of Frederick. Local men served in regiments of the Maryland National Guard, and a federal recruiting office at Union Hall on South Carroll Street was established where men enlisted for three-year tours of duty in the Independent Brigade of Maryland Volunteers. Union Hall and the B&O Railroad freight depot were used to store military supplies and munitions. By the end of 1861, Frederick hosted 15,000 Union troops, as well as the headquarters of the Army of the Potomac. Union troops were commanded by General Nathaniel Banks. He occupied the former residence of Confederate supporter Bradley T. Johnson, who had left Frederick to fight for the South. Diarist Jacob Engelbrecht wrote that the city was "chuck full of soldiers." According to newspaper reports, soldiers filled the streets. Residents heard:

> the notes of the drum and fife, the inspiriting bugle, and music from military bands, the brilliant and varied military costumes and the rush of ladies attracted by the gay sight and tempted forth by the balmy atmosphere. . . . [It added] a strange and exciting aspect to the town, and it is difficult in the din and apparent confusion to recognize its identity. Business is brisk.

Kemp Hall was the headquarters of the provost marshal, the town's military leader, and also served as a military supply depot for 500 wagonloads of supplies. Troops camped at the fairgrounds on East Patrick Street. The Fourth Connecticut Regiment invited the public to watch its dress parades at 6 a.m. and 5 p.m. at the barracks on

FREDERICK

South Market Street. Military supplies included 1,000 mules located on a farm near the south side of the barracks. In mid-October, crowds gathered to watch the First Maryland Regiment march through Frederick on its way to Darnestown. Local supporters of the Confederacy also enlisted to fight. Captain Bradley T. Johnson, a Frederick resident, joined the Confederate forces at Harper's Ferry, Virginia, with a company he formed of Frederick County men.

The presence of the soldiers boosted the local economy. The U.S. Bakery opened in December at the southeast corner of Market and Third Streets and could bake enough bread to feed 20,000 men daily. Two stores, on East Patrick and West Patrick, sold military equipment such as swords, uniform hats, and uniform accessories. Children could buy games related to the Civil War at Smith's News Depot and Variety Store. Prostitution was practiced, even though city ordinance prohibited it and the provost marshal tried to stop it. Some commerce was not to the benefit of the soldiers. A few residents were repeatedly requested to stop selling liquor to the soldiers, who were dying of intoxication.

Frederick residents witnessed the hell of war when the Union Military Hospital was established here in August 1861. Dr. W.A. Hammond, the assistant surgeon of the U.S. Army, was in charge of the hospital. Frederick County already had been designated a medical supply depot in 1859, when the federal government rented a warehouse on Carroll Street to store medical supplies. With the establishment of the hospital, the Medical Purveyor's Depot was moved from Hagerstown to Frederick. The hospital, located at the barracks on South Market Street, was one of the Union's largest. Frederick was an ideal location because it was located along railroad lines, it was near Baltimore and Washington, and it had paved streets, water service, and gas lighting. The hospital was moved to Baltimore in late August but was returned to Frederick in December. In March 1862, the hospital served 653 patients. By July, as fighting increased, the hospital was caring for more than 1,000 patients. Many funeral processions traveled south on Market Street from the hospital to Mount Olivet Cemetery, located only a few blocks south.

The work of The Ladies Relief Association, formed by the women of Frederick in August 1861 to tend to the sick and wounded of both sides, was essential to the care of the patients. The association president was Mrs. Gideon Bantz. Dorothy L. Dix, superintendent of army nurses, visited the hospital in January 1862 to observe the quality of care that the ladies provided to the soldiers.

The Confederate Army advanced into Maryland in late summer 1862. Confederate General Robert E. Lee sought to bring the war into Union territory and thus force a settlement with the South. He also hoped that victories in the North would help the South gain credibility with England and France, who were potential Confederate allies. Lee anticipated that hundreds of Frederick County secessionists would welcome the chance to join the Confederate Army. Confederate troops began crossing the Potomac River on September 4, 1862, and moved toward Frederick with relative ease. General Stonewall Jackson's troops also traveled toward Frederick from Point of Rocks, destroying telegraph lines and ripping up B&O Railroad tracks as they went. Residents of southern Frederick County, including about 20 boatmen and their mules from the Chesapeake and Ohio Canal, fled to Frederick and warned of the pending invasion. The Confederates were camped outside the city two days later, on September 8. Only one Union military company, part of the Potomac Home Brigade, remained in the city. All other military officials and many citizens had fled to Baltimore or Pennsylvania, taking their valuables with them. When invasion was imminent, the Potomac Home Brigade commander, Captain William T. Faithful, mobilized into action along with two remaining military officials, Assistant Surgeon of the Army Dr. R.F. Weir, the head of the military hospital; and Assistant Quartermaster Lieutenant G. Castle. They were joined by the local B&O agent, John T. Quinn. Valuable military and medical supplies and 300 hospital patients were loaded on all railroad cars that Quinn could secure and sent to Pennsylvania. The Union contingent then burned the non-critical supplies to prevent them from falling into Confederate hands. Faithful ordered the local telegraph operator to disable his instruments and flee to Pennsylvania. He then assembled and marched his troops to Knoxville, in southwestern Frederick County, as his commander at Harper's Ferry had ordered. Faithful had been ordered to simply destroy the Union property. The group spent an additional five hours gathering supplies and sending them to Pennsylvania, thus saving the government hundreds of thousands of dollars. It was a harrowing escape. Arriving Confederate troops shot at Assistant Quartermaster Castle as he escaped on horseback.

When the 80,000 member-strong Confederate Army entered the city, martial law was declared, and native son Colonel Bradley T. Johnson was appointed provost marshal. The Confederates lowered all United States flags and raised their own flags. They occupied the train depot, hotels, and liquor stores. General Jackson attended services at the Reformed Church on Sunday, September 7, the day after the troops reached Frederick. He intended to attend Presbyterian services, but they were not available. Apparently, Jackson fell asleep during the Reformed service. Two days after their arrival, on September 8, Johnson issued a call for southern supporters to enlist in the Confederate Army; few responded. Frederick residents gave the Confederates a reception that ranged from cordial to cool. Businesses closed once merchants saw that the soldiers paid for purchases with Confederate scrip. Residents showed little enthusiasm for the presence of the "unwashed and odoriferous" raggedly dressed soldiers. Some supporters quietly showed their enthusiasm by visiting Jackson, Lee, and other officials or by giving supplies to the soldiers. Overall, Frederick's chilly reception was anti-climactic for the Confederates.

It was during this invasion that elderly resident Barbara Fritchie's dramatic defense of the United States flag under threat from Confederate General Stonewall Jackson supposedly occurred, as immortalized by poet John Greenleaf Whittier. According to Whittier's famous poem, Jackson marched into Frederick and ordered his soldiers to halt when he reached Fritchie's West Patrick Street home and saw the flag flying in her attic window. He ordered that the flag be shot at, but as soon as it was, the 96-year-old Fritchie angrily reached out the window and grabbed the "silken scarf" before it fell to the ground. According to the most climactic line in the poem, Fritchie shook the flag at the Confederate general and sternly dressed him down: " 'Shoot, if you must, this old gray head,/But spare your country's flag,' she said." Her command awakened in Jackson some slumbering pride for his former country. Ashamed at his earlier order, he instructed his men, " 'Who touches a hair of yon gray head/Dies like a dog! March on!' he said." The flag continued to fly above the heads of the Confederate soldiers as they marched through the town.

"The Ballad of Barbara Freitchie" (Whittier spelled her last name with an additional "e") was published in the October 1863 issue of *Atlantic Monthly* magazine. Fritchie died on December 18, 1862 with no knowledge of the poem that established her place in Civil War folklore and that would be recited by generations of schoolchildren. For nearly as long as the poem has been around, generations of historians and other curious people have questioned whether the events depicted in the poem ever actually happened.

One fact is unquestioned: Barbara Fritchie did live in Frederick. She was born Barbara Hauer in 1766 in Lancaster, Pennsylvania, the daughter of German immigrants. The family moved to Frederick and lived in a small house on West Patrick Street on the banks of Carroll Creek east of Bentz Street. Legend has it that as a young woman she served coffee to President Washington at a local tavern. In 1806, at the age of 40, Barbara married John Casper Fritchie, whose father, Casper, was executed in 1780 for his part in a Loyalist plot to free British prisoners. The couple had no children. John Fritchie died of cholera in 1849, leaving Barbara a widow. One interesting historical footnote is that Mrs. Fritchie is listed as a slaveowner in the 1850 federal slave census. A 48-year-old black man and an 11-year-old mulatto girl were in bondage to her. When the Confederate Army invaded Frederick in September 1862, she was 96 and not in the best of health.

According to the recollection of Fritchie's niece, some interaction might have occurred between Fritchie and Confederate soldiers. As reported by Richard Lebherz in the March 1988 issue of *Diversions* magazine, Fritchie's niece, Caroline Ebert, told the story to her friend, Emma Southworth of Washington, D.C., a popular novelist. Southworth relayed the story to Whittier. According to Ebert's account, Fritchie either was told that soldiers were marching along her street, or she heard the sound of marching feet. Thinking the Union Army had arrived, Fritchie grabbed a flag and went out to the porch. A Confederate soldier called out, "Give me your flag, Granny, and I'll stick it on my horse's head." Fritchie refused, and another soldier cried out, "Shoot her damned head off." But an officer rode up and said something similar to what later appeared in Whittier's poem: "If you harm a hair on her head, I'll shoot you down like a dog." Apparently, Fritchie's niece told the novelist Southworth of the incident, and the novelist wrote about it to Whittier. With more than a bit of poetic license—for instance, the anonymous Confederate officer became Stonewall Jackson—Whittier transformed the event into his ballad.

Others contend that no incident between Fritchie and the Confederate soldiers could have happened. Diarist Jacob Engelbrecht, who lived across the street from Fritchie, watched the Confederates pass down the street, "nearly continually looking at the Rebel Army passing the door." He claimed that when Lee's army passed Fritchie's house, he witnessed no incident similar to that described in Whittier's poem. "I do not believe one word of it," he reported in his diary on April 8, 1869, the date that Fritchie's house was demolished to widen Carroll Creek. In his discussion of the incident, J. Thomas Scharf cited others who discounted Whittier's poem, including a member of Jackson's staff. Scharf himself took issue with the story, pointing out that the Confederates marched through before dawn, not at noon as the poem states. At this early hour, the elderly Fritchie might have been awake and installed her flag since, Scharf said, "As a rule, persons of Mrs. Fritchie's age, as Mr. Whittier has forgotten, are the earliest risers." However, Scharf contended that it would have been too dark for anyone to see the flag. Scharf also took issue with Whittier's portrayal of Jackson as easily swayed by the sight of the U.S. flag and willing to waste ammunition to shoot it.

In the end, perhaps the facts are not as important as the sentiments. "What is extraordinary," according to a summary of the story in *Windows on Frederick,* the 2001 compilation of Richard Lebherz's work, "is that this 96-year-old, comparatively insignificant woman was plucked out of obscurity and turned into a national heroine by a poet who had never even met her." The more cynical say we should not bother to question the story's authenticity, because the publicity has been so extensive that nothing can stop the story from spreading. British Prime Minister Winston Churchill recited the poem during a visit to the replica Barbara Fritchie house on May 17, 1943. Even in 1882, when Scharf was writing, Fritchie was well-known. "As long as the name of Frederick City lasts the poem of Barbara Freitchie will be quoted in connection with it," Scharf wrote. "This is immortality—not of place, but of the poet's gift. It is part of the poet's power. He suffers, starves, is ignored, condemned, but something in his lines survives him, and that something, be it correct or incorrect, is too strong for criticism."

On September 10, the Confederates began leaving Frederick to head west, as Union General George B. McClellan's forces moved toward Frederick. In contrast to the cool reception to the Confederate invasion, Frederick residents were ecstatic to see the Union forces when they arrived on September 12 on the heels of the Confederates. According to an observer quoted in Williams's *History of Frederick County, Maryland,* "Women blessed God and the soldiers, and rushed out to kiss the old flag; gray-haired men hobbled forth with radiant faces, and the young shouted their welcome, while children capered in holiday glee. The line had not been five minutes in the street before national banners, large and little, were flung from the windows, and draped with inspiring grace almost every threshold."

On September 14, Union and Confederate forces clashed west of Frederick at South Mountain, a battle so loud that it was heard in Frederick. Two days later, the two forces met again at Sharpsburg, Maryland, along Antietam Creek 20 miles west of Frederick. Known as the Battle of Antietam, the engagement was the bloodiest single day of battle in the war, with 22,000 casualties. The Union forces won, but in the process lost 12,000 troops to the Confederates' 10,000.

Many of the wounded were transported to Frederick, which became "one vast hospital," in the words of the *Philadelphia Inquirer.* Nearly 10,000 Confederate and Union wounded were treated in Frederick or transported here temporarily until they could be moved to military hospitals in other cities. "On September 27 alone, 142 ambulances arrived with 800 wounded transferred from hospitals near the battlefield," according to Terry Reimer's 2001 book, *One Vast Hospital: The Civil War Hospital Sites in Frederick, Maryland after Antietam.* According to Reimer, in fall 1862, the number of wounded in Frederick equaled the number of residents. Seven general hospitals were established, comprising 27 buildings and two camps. Several other buildings and private homes also were used to house the wounded. In addition to the existing hospital at the barracks, buildings pressed into service as hospitals included most of the city's churches, as well as schools, hotels, and public halls.

The influx of wounded and medical personnel brought both the exciting buzz of activity and the gruesome spectacle of war. According to Reimer, letters from male nurses stationed in Frederick praised the town's attractions, such as "oysters and lager beer" and "some of the prettiest gals in this town you ever seen, golly but they do like the soldiers." Some residents probably enjoyed the visitors from many parts of the country. Meanwhile, in his diary entry for October 29, 1862, Engelbrecht reported his encounters with the horrors and realities of war. "Wounded Soldiers—our Streets are full of Wounded Soldiers, many of them with one arm off, yesterday I met two on the Street the one had his right arm off & the other had his left arm off & another in Company wounded on the Knee, walking with two Crutches."

Most of the hospitals were returned to their owners by January 1863; the two hospital camps on the outskirts of town were closed in March. Only General Hospital #1, at the barracks, remained in use throughout the war. A few other buildings in town were used for overflow or for storing supplies, including Coppersmith Hall at the northwest corner of Market and Church Streets, the three schoolhouses, and the old German Reformed Church.

Two weeks after the Battles of South Mountain and Antietam, President Lincoln arrived in Frederick October 1 on his way to tour the battlefields and to visit General McClellan. The President and his party stopped in Frederick on his return to Washington. Crowds thronged West Patrick Street to welcome him, and a Presidential salute was fired by Battery K of the First New York Artillery. Even a blustery rainstorm did not discourage the crowd. Lincoln proceeded north toward the Record Street home of Mrs. Ramsey, where General George L. Hartsuff was recuperating from wounds received at Antietam.

Before departing by train from the B&O Railroad station, on the southeast corner of Market and All Saints Streets, Lincoln addressed the town. He emphasized that it was not his place to give a speech but only to thank the soldiers and citizens for their devotion to the Union cause. He said he had no malice in his heart toward those engaged in rebellion. In his final words, he expressed the hope that the country would be united once again: "May our children, and our children's children, for a thousand generations, continue to enjoy the benefits conferred upon us by a united country, and have cause yet to rejoice under those glorious institutions bequeathed us by Washington and his compeers!"

The Civil War

Confederate troops entered Maryland a second time shortly after Antietam. General J.E.B. Stuart and his troops crossed the Potomac above Williamsport, in Washington County west of Frederick, and disrupted transportation and communication lines as they moved east. They passed through Frederick County and were turned back to Virginia at Poolesville, in Montgomery County. Even though the conflict had moved south by the end of 1862, Frederick and the surrounding county still housed troops and wounded soldiers. In June 1863, a looming invasion sent Frederick residents into another panic. Confederate troops entered Maryland a third time on their way to invade Pennsylvania. Residents fled on trains to Baltimore, and free blacks feared that the invading Confederates would kidnap them and sell them into slavery in the South. Government property was moved out of the city, and the hospital patients who could be moved were evacuated. The Federal Army was stationed just outside Frederick. Despite the preparations and fears, no major military activity occurred in the city, aside from a few Confederate cavalry chasing Union troops east through Frederick along Patrick Street, and Union troops pursuing Confederates on South Market Street. The real fighting occurred July 1–3 in Gettysburg, Pennsylvania, in a battle that turned the momentum of the war in favor of the Union. The barracks hospital received wounded soldiers from this battle.

After Gettysburg, the war continued to touch the city of Frederick. In August 1863, a Colonel Creager was arrested after enlisting slaves in the U.S. Army. He had encouraged at least 50 slaves from all over Frederick County to desert their masters and enlist. This was not uncommon, apparently. While one civilian recruiter was being held in jail in Frederick, a group of slave prisoners learned he was there and smuggled him a note saying they wanted to enlist. In October, a group of Confederate deserters captured in Frederick agreed to take the oath of allegiance and were released. A Christmas 1863 celebration at the hospital featured decorations, a minstrel group, a band, and many local residents. A parade and public dinner were held in Frederick in February 1864 for Cole's Rangers, who were furloughed in the city.

For a fourth time, in July 1864, the front lines of the war threatened to reach Frederick. Confederate General Robert E. Lee planned an invasion of Maryland to capture Washington and draw Union General Ulysses S. Grant away from his advance on Richmond. On July 7, Frederick residents were alarmed to learn that the Confederate Army, led by General Jubal A. Early, was not far away. His army met Union troops at Middletown and pushed them back to Frederick. The Confederates intended to come to Frederick and occupy the city. This appears to have been the most terrifying time of the war for Frederick residents, as the Confederates were embittered over Union tactics in the South.

Over the next two days, the Confederates entered Frederick from the west and the south. More Union troops were sent here, but were repelled and withdrew. Once again, residents fled, businesses closed, government property was removed, the B&O Railroad removed its equipment, and the banks withdrew most of their funds. On July 9, the Confederates delivered a letter to the Mayor of Frederick demanding flour, sugar, coffee, salt, and bacon. More ominously, another letter the same day demanded $200,000 cash or the equivalent in medical supplies, food, ordnance, and other supplies. Meanwhile, Confederate troops obtained food and other supplies in town. Unlike the troops who entered Frederick two years earlier, this wave generally refused to pay for supplies. City officials decided to respond as quickly as possible to the ransom demand, for fear of reprisal. The banks quickly cooperated and loaned the cash, which was delivered in baskets to a wagon sent by the Confederates. The Confederates provided a receipt to complete the transaction. The city did not pay off the ransom loan until 1951. The city continually requested reimbursement from Congress. After one effort, a House of Representatives report issued in 1874 stated that it was commonly known that nations do not reimburse citizens for wartime damages caused by an enemy. Undaunted, Frederick continued to seek reimbursement, even as recently as 1986. Maryland's congressional delegation continues to seek reimbursement from the U.S. Treasury.

After receiving the ransom, General Early and his troops left Frederick and headed southeast toward Washington, intending to take the city. Union General Lew Wallace and 5,000 troops were waiting in a 6-mile line along the Monocacy River. It was at this location, only a few miles south of Frederick, that the Battle of the Monocacy was fought. Often overlooked by historians, the battle is important because it bought time to reinforce the Union capital. Even though the Confederates won, the Battle of the Monocacy delayed their march on Washington, thus providing General Grant time to fortify the city. As a result, instead of targeting Washington, Early moved south to Virginia at Poolesville.

After the Battle of the Monocacy, it became clear that the war had turned to the North's favor. After learning that southern sympathizers had furnished troop information to the Confederates, Union troops in Frederick began punishing them. All male citizens were required to pledge allegiance to the Union, and any who refused were imprisoned and their property was seized. In October 1864, Maryland residents approved a new state constitution that eliminated slavery. The war ended on April 9, 1865, when Robert E. Lee surrendered the Army of Northern Virginia to Ulysses S. Grant at Appomattox, Virginia. Lee did not surrender all Confederate armies, but the war was effectively over. Joyous Frederick residents thronged the streets. Military bands played, church bells rung, flags decorated the city, and homes were illuminated long into the night. The Army General Hospital at the barracks remained open until mid-September. On September 14, the government auctioned its remaining medical supplies and hospital property.

Just six days after Lee's surrender, on April 15, joy turned to shock and grief with the death of President Lincoln. He had been shot the previous night by John Wilkes Booth while attending a play at Ford's Theater in Washington. Frederick's mayor immediately closed businesses for the day and asked local churches to hold services. Frederick residents mourned on April 18 by tolling bells, closing businesses, and holding church services. According to an editorial in the local weekly newspaper *The Examiner*, "Large congregations were in attendance and testified by their tearful eyes and devout demeanor how keenly and intensely they felt the agonizing calamity that had so suddenly overwhelmed them with grief too deep and profound for utterance and that brought to every heart a painful realization of the terrible reality."

Chapter Five

REBUILDING AND MODERNIZATION

(1870s–1915)

The Civil War officially ended in May 1865 when the last "Rebel" army surrendered, in Texas. "This closes . . . this wicked and sinful rebellion, which has agitated the United States for more than four years, and I do hope another such a rebellion will never be tried again," Engelbrecht wrote in his diary May 31.

The majority of Frederick residents probably agreed with Engelbrecht's sentiment. They wanted to move beyond war and return to normal life. Both Confederate and Union soldiers came back to town. Local businesses sought to resume operations. Area farmers with damaged crops wanted to recoup their losses. Infrastructure such as railroad tracks and telegraph lines needed to be repaired. As Frederick struggled to recover from the war, technology and industrial development contributed to the city's growth and prosperity.

Locally, the return to normalcy began quickly after the war, and optimism was high. Although not intended as such, one event symbolized the transition to peace, in a small way. The Maryland School for the Deaf was founded in 1867 next to the former barracks on South Market Street, which no longer quartered troops. The school opened in 1868 as the Maryland Deaf and Dumb Institute. It operated inside the barracks until the school's buildings were opened in 1873. The school's original 30-member Board of Visitors, its governing body, represented every county in the state. One of the three barracks buildings was demolished in 1874 to make room for school expansion. Williams reported in *History of Frederick County, Maryland* that the school taught the "Combined Method," in which students learned both speech and lip reading. Students also learned sign language and writing, as well as industrial skills such as printing, shoemaking, and cabinetmaking. Reflecting the reality of life in the late nineteenth century, the school was open only to white students.

Only three years after the war, residents once again enjoyed the annual agricultural fair that had been held at the barracks since 1853. The state was using the barracks grounds for the School for the Deaf, and the Frederick County Agricultural Society, the fair sponsor, was forced to find a new location. The society raised funds in 1867 to purchase land on the east side of the city for a fairgrounds. In September, the society bought 14 acres on the north side of the Baltimore Turnpike east of East Street from General Edward Shriver, and an adjacent parcel from William Falconer, both of whom owned large parcels in that area. The first fair since 1860 was held on these grounds. The society bought more land in 1875, increasing the fairgrounds to

33 acres. As of 1873, when the fairgrounds were depicted on a map of the city, the fairgrounds consisted of stalls along most of the perimeter, a half-mile racetrack, a pavilion, a judging stand, and three entry gates. Photos from the period showed that the fair was a popular event, attracting large crowds of well-dressed people. Presidents Ulysses S. Grant and Rutherford B. Hayes visited the fair during their terms in office.

Frederick's African-American residents found reason to celebrate in 1870. On March 30, the federal government announced that the 15th Amendment, granting suffrage to all male citizens regardless of race, was ratified and made part of the Constitution. The amendment complemented an 1867 state law granting the vote to black males in Maryland. Engelbrecht noted that the "colored citizens" of Frederick County celebrated the new amendment in June 1870 with a picnic about 3 miles from Frederick. They formed a mile-long procession through the city as they marched toward the picnic grounds. The passage of the 15th Amendment followed the passage of the 13th Amendment, which outlawed slavery, and the passage of the 14th Amendment, which gave citizenship to blacks. Five years earlier, in 1865, African Americans and whites already had celebrated the 1863 Emancipation Proclamation with an all-day event at Howard's Woods just southwest of Frederick (the war made it impossible to celebrate until 1865).

By 1873, Frederick residents could spend an evening at the opera. The city government constructed a combined city hall and theater known as the City Opera House. It housed the second largest stage in the state and featured performances such as operas, Shakespearean dramas, and shows such as the George White Scandals. John Philip Sousa and his 66-piece orchestra attracted a sellout crowd to the Opera House in 1897. The building was remodeled in 1963 to enlarge City Hall and build a parking deck, and that building now houses Brewer's Alley restaurant.

Growth and prosperity characterized Frederick throughout the late nineteenth century and early twentieth century. Immigrants and other new residents contributed to the city's population expansion. Newly constructed train and trolley lines facilitated transportation through the city and linked it with rural areas, new industries developed, more schools were built, and new community institutions were established.

With the end of the Civil War in 1865, the United States resumed its position as a haven for immigrants. From the 1870s to the 1920s, immigrants poured into the United States, especially from southern and eastern Europe. Some of the new residents made their homes in Frederick. According to the 1870 and 1880 federal censuses, immigrants to Frederick hailed mainly from Germany, as they had historically. Many of Frederick's immigrants also came from Ireland. Other countries represented by Frederick residents were England, Switzerland, Holland, Poland, France, and Scotland.

The growing popularity of railroad transportation after the war benefited Frederick. New train and trolley lines increased transportation options for residents of the city and the rural areas of the county. The transportation of people and goods, such as farm produce, was cheaper and faster. In 1872, the Frederick and Pennsylvania Line Railroad was the first new line installed since the B&O arrived in 1831. The city of Frederick built the railroad to connect to the Western Maryland Railroad line in Carroll County, and to lines in Pennsylvania. The station was located on East Street between Patrick and Church Streets. Frederick leased the line to the Pennsylvania Railroad, which bought the line in 1896. The line originated south of All Saints Street at the B&O line and extended north on East Street.

The next year, in 1873, train travel to Washington became available. It was 20 years in the making. Plans began in 1853 when the Metropolitan Railroad Company was organized, but the tracks never were built. Twenty years later, the Baltimore and Ohio Railroad pursued the idea and built tracks to Point of Rocks, in southern Frederick County. From there, tracks were constructed north to Frederick Junction. From there, passengers could take the northern branch of the main line into downtown Frederick. Service was provided until 1949.

Residents west of Frederick wanted train service so that they could travel to Frederick and ship farm goods to market. Several attempts were made to extend train service west, including an 1853 effort to extend a railroad from Washington, D.C. to Hagerstown and the 1884 formation of the Frederick & Middletown Railroad. A major obstacle to extending a railroad west was Catoctin Mountain, whose high elevation made the operation of steam trains difficult. Then, in April 1893, the Frederick & Middletown Passenger Railroad was organized by a group of private investors led by George W. Smith, a wealthy farmer. The organization reincorporated a year later as the Frederick & Middletown Railway so that the line also could carry freight, in case passenger service was not profitable. Through various mergers and acquisitions, this company eventually operated all of the trolley lines that operated within Frederick and that offered service to Hagerstown and Thurmont.

Construction of the electric trolley line began in spring 1896. The line originated at Carroll and Patrick Streets and extended west to Braddock Heights by August and to Middletown by October. Soon, it was clear that both the freight and passenger service would be very profitable. To attract additional train customers, the company built a dance pavilion and observatory at Braddock Heights, ensuring steady business. And once the service was running regularly, farmers in the Middletown Valley stopped hauling their produce over the mountain by wagon teams.

The railway got off to an alarming start. After some trial runs, two trolleys were put into service to Braddock Heights on August 23. Thousands of Frederick citizens rode the trolleys to the mountaintop resort, and at the end of the day, railway President George W. Smith and 109 people boarded a train car that could only hold 48 people. On its way down the mountain, motorman William Mantz lost control and the speeding trolley derailed and crashed into a field. The accident resulted in serious injuries and one woman was killed. The accident prompted the company to implement strict safety measures, but it did not harm the railway's business. The company built a car barn in 1896 at Patrick and Carroll, and in 1897 it stopped buying power from Frederick Light & Power Co. and built its own power plant. In 1904, trolley service extended from Middletown to Hagerstown through connecting lines operated by other companies. Trolleys also carried passengers east to the fairgrounds. Construction was completed on October 12, 1896 on the Frederick City Suburban Railway, which transported 15,000 passengers to the fair that fall. The company later was acquired by the Frederick & Middletown Railway.

In 1905, the Frederick & Middletown Railway itself was taken over, in a move by a group of Baltimore businessmen to extend a fast electric line from Baltimore to Hagerstown. Local interests repurchased the company in 1908.

Meanwhile, train service also was extended north to Thurmont. A steam line, the Washington, Frederick, and Gettysburg Railway Company, began service on January 1, 1909 from Fifth Street. Later that year, some of the region's railroad operations were consolidated into the Frederick Railroad Company, which was a merger of the Frederick & Middletown Railway, the steam line, and the Jefferson & Braddock Heights Railway Company. The steam line to Thurmont was electrified. Now one company, the Frederick Railroad Company, operated all trains to Thurmont, Middletown, and Jefferson.

In 1913, railroad ownership was consolidated further when the Frederick Railroad Company acquired the Hagerstown Railway, which owned the rail line from Hagerstown to Middletown. With this acquisition, the Frederick Railroad Company extended its western service to Hagerstown and also changed its name to the Hagerstown & Frederick Railway. Eventually, the company became Potomac Edison, which ran the electric trolley lines, sold power from its plants, and owned and operated bus lines through the Blue Ridge Transportation Company starting in 1924. Trolley service ended in 1954. The trolley station building now houses the offices of *The Frederick News-Post* newspaper.

Another section of Frederick's public services that grew after the Civil War was the school system. The first recognized school for black students in Frederick County was located in the basement of Quinn Chapel on East Third Street. African-American students also were taught at Asbury Methodist Episcopal Church. In 1872, every Board of Education in Maryland was required to establish a minimum of one school in each election district for black students. In the 1880s, two more buildings were built to serve Frederick black students, West Seventh Street School and South Bentz Street School. Among the principals of West Seventh Street School was John W. Bruner, who began teaching in 1899 in Walkersville and later became West Seventh Street School's principal. He also was supervisor of black schools in Frederick County. Bruner retired in 1940. South Bentz Street School held a night school, begun in 1917 for teenagers older than 16 who worked during the day. Prior to the establishment of the local night school, students were forced to travel to Virginia to attend the Hampton Institute's high school division.

Black students now had their own schools, but the facilities were inferior to the schools serving white students. Blacks were required to attend school for only 100 days, from November to mid-April, to coincide with the farming season. The "colored" schools were heated with stoves that burned smoky, cheap, soft coal. White schools used more expensive hard coal. Black students studied from textbooks no longer needed by the white schools. Teachers were resourceful and provided quality education using the resources they had. One revered educator during this period was Esther Grinage, who taught elementary students for 35 years. The kindergarten established in the Pythian Castle was named in her honor.

A girls high school opened in Frederick in 1889 when a veteran educator of several Maryland girls schools came to town. Margaret Minerva Robinson opened the school on East Church Street. Robinson previously founded schools in Berlin on the Eastern Shore and in Baltimore and Harford Counties. When the East Church Street school opened, Robinon was the only teacher. By her retirement in 1906, the school's faculty numbered 12. During her tenure, the deteriorated first building was torn down in 1900, and a new building was built for an estimated $23,000. The building contained 12 classrooms, a teacher's room, a library, and two bathrooms. The building became Church Street School after the new, coed Frederick High School was established at Elm Street in 1922. Today, the Church Street building houses the headquarters of the Frederick County Board of Education.

A high school education became possible for Frederick's young men when Boys High School opened in 1891 at Koontz Hall at 314 N. Market Street. Amon Burgee, a native of southern Frederick County, became principal in September 1894. Burgee, who at first was the school's only teacher as well as its principal, soon earned the respect of the students and the parents for his high standards. He assigned nightly homework, added a fourth year of study, and established a literary society. Many colleges and universities accredited the high school, so graduates were not required to take entrance exams. Burgee led the school through its 1896 move to 520 N. Market Street, where a six-room brick school had been built on the site of Primary School 72, and through a second move in 1912 to Elm Street at Park Avenue, near Frederick Memorial Hospital. Burgee retired in 1917, two years before military uniforms were adopted and five years before the school merged with Girls High School. Burgee was always an honored guest at the Boys High School reunions, until his death in 1945.

Higher education for women was offered in 1893, when the Frederick Female Seminary on East Church Street became the Woman's College. The seminary board of directors leased the buildings to the Potomac Synod of the Reformed Church to establish the college. The college opened in fall 1893 with 112 students from six states. In 1913, seminary graduate Margaret Scholl Hood established a substantial endowment and donated 45 acres on the northwest side of the city to relocate the growing college. The college occupies the site today and has been renamed Hood College in honor of its benefactor.

Other schools in operation included the girls primary school on N. Market Street, which operated until 1877; Jail Street School at 101 W. South Street, which was a primary school until 1913; and Primary School 72 at 520 N. Market Street. Primary School 72 became Primary School 9 in the 1870s and was demolished in 1895 to make way for Boys High School. Classes were moved to the Etchison Building on West Patrick Street. Primary School 9 was probably the school that the Frederick County grand jury inspected in February 1894. According to the inspection report, the school, which it called "the public school house on North Market Street," was found to be "substantial enough in structure in that respect neither dangerous to the safety or health of the children, but it is old and inadequate for the accommodation and comfort of the pupils." Just a year later, however, a local newspaper called the building "the old barn-like structure masquerading as a school."

Businesses and industries continued to develop after the Civil War. Some older industries continued to flourish, while new industries organized to address changing consumer needs. According to an 1873 business directory, for instance, tanneries, mills, dry goods merchants, wagon makers, and saddle and harness makers continued to operate in Frederick as they had for more than a century. Tanneries were located along Carroll Creek. Philip B. Kunkel's tannery occupied the north side of Carroll Creek east of Carroll Street, in the same location as John Kunkel, as depicted on an 1853 map. The two Kunkels likely were related and probably were father and son. George K. Birely's tannery was directly east, on a site that it occupied since at least 1853. Gideon Bantz still operated a tannery north of Carroll Creek and west of Court Street. John Loats, a substantial landowner south of the Maryland School for the Deaf, operated a tannery there. Six years later, in 1879, Loats was known for the orphanage he established on East Church Street. Today the building houses the Historical Society of Frederick County.

The city's two flour mills also operated along Carroll Creek. In 1873, Lewis Bruner operated the flour mill on Bentz Street that was founded by Jacob Bentz in the late 1700s. Newton Zentz purchased this mill in 1895; it burned down in 1928 and the site became part of Baker Park. Also in 1873, William Kemp's mill was located on the other side of the city, on the east side of Carroll Street, south of Carroll Creek and north of the B&O freight depot. Kemp started the mill in the early 1870s. A fire destroyed the original stone building in 1893, and it was replaced with a four-story brick building. After the Mountain City Milling Co. bought it in 1899, the mill became known as Mountain City Mill. Another fire struck, destroying the mill in 1906. Yet another mill was erected in 1907, and by the 1930s it was used for grain storage. It was sold to the Great Southern Printing and Manufacturing Co. in 1958. The company, publisher of the *Frederick News* and *Frederick Post*, stored large rolls of newsprint in it. The company donated the building to the city for a visual arts center, which opened in 1993.

Dry goods and groceries were a staple of the Frederick business community, as they had been practically since Frederick's beginnings. The 1873 business directory listed four, all along Market and Patrick Streets. Wagonmaking and saddle and harness making would become obsolete within 40 years, but they still flourished in 1873. Three wagon or carriage manufacturers and one saddle and harness manufacturer operated in Frederick. Other longtime industries included iron foundries and blacksmiths.

Several new manufacturers began operations in Frederick in the late nineteenth century. In 1869, Lewis McMurray founded a corn and tomato packing factory at the southeast corner of West All Saints and South Bentz Streets. His business thrived, and by 1886 he was packing three million cans of corn a year and added beans and peas. McMurray bought produce from farmers and also grew his own produce on 3,000 acres that he owned near Frederick. He packed so much produce that wagons full of corn frequently stretched from Bentz to Market, waiting to be unloaded. The company employed many local men and women, as well as children. Hoping for the same success, Aaron and Joseph Rosenstock established the Frederick City Packing Company in 1891.

Five businessmen established the Frederick Seamless Hosiery Company in 1887 at the corner of East Patrick and North Wisner Streets. Williams, writing in his *History of Frederick County, Maryland*, claimed that one of the reasons these men started the company was to dispel the stereotype that it was dishonorable for women to work outside the home. The men were "ever alert to advance the interest of Frederick as well as being deeply concerned in the betterment of the condition of its girls, influenced almost entirely by motives of philanthropy."

The hosiery company began with 18 knitting machines. It was difficult at first to convince the female employees that work was dignified and would provide independence, but gradually they were won over. Within two years, the company's customer base grew to such an extent that larger facilities were needed. The company merged with Union Manufacturing Co., and the new company purchased a large tract of land and built two mills and a dye house. For a few months the company added shirts to its product line, but that proved unsuccessful and was abandoned. By 1910, the company employed 300 people.

The Palmetto Fibre Brush Company was established in 1890 on West South Street. In the early 1900s, the company's name was changed to Ox Fibre Brush Company and operations were relocated to the south side of East Church Street, east of East Street. The 12-acre plant employed more than 300 men and boys in its production of fiber brushes, using equipment invented by the company's vice president, McClintock Young. Fibers were shipped to Frederick from various points around the world, treated, cleaned, and stapled to wooden backs. Then the fibers were trimmed and the backs were polished and varnished. As of 1910, the company manufactured 12 million brushes a year.

One of the two newspapers that became today's *Frederick News-Post* was started on October 15, 1883. *The News,* a five-column, four-page broadsheet, was founded by partners William Theodore Delaplaine, Thomas Schley, and Victor Marken. The three partners formed a printing company in 1880 in the MacGill Building on South Market Street. The printing company moved to a larger location at the northwest corner of Patrick and Court Streets and put out its first issue of *The News* in the upper floors of the Whalen Building at 4 through 10 N. Market Street. The newspaper began as a morning paper, but it became an evening paper by January 1884. Two months after *The News* debuted, the company began a weekly paper that became *The Semi-Weekly News* in 1888, and was published until December 1953. The growing company, which no longer included Marken, incorporated as The Great Southern

Printing and Manufacturing Company in 1888 and moved to the Mutual Insurance Company building at 44 N. Market Street. In 1916, the company bought out a rival daily paper, *The Post*, based on North Court Street. The company moved to this building and remained there until 1968, when it relocated to its present location at the former trolley barn at the southeast corner of Carroll and Patrick Streets. The company published the two newspapers separately, *The Frederick Post* in the morning and *The Frederick News* as an afternoon paper. The two papers merged to create *The Frederick News-Post*, on June 1, 2002.

Many Frederick County dairy farmers sold their milk to the Baltimore and Washington White Cross Milk Company, which opened near the B&O Railroad freight depot in 1909. The operation was capable of handling and storing 10,000 gallons of milk daily. Milk was concentrated to remove the water, housed in cold storage, loaded into refrigerated train cars, and transported directly from the plant to Baltimore and Washington. This operation was not the only dairy in Frederick; the Excelsior Sanitary Dairy operated in the late 1800s on East Seventh Street. Today, the building houses the Dairy Maid Dairy.

Other local industries included Frederick Steam Brick Works; Frederick Shutter Fastener factory; Frederick City Manufacturing Company, which made inks and medicine; Economy Silo and Tank Company; Excelsior Steam Carpet Cleaning Works; Ramsburg Fertilizer Company; M.J. Grove Lime Company; Hygeia Ice Factory; and Holzman Manufacturing Company, which made ladies' shirt waists. There also were cigar factories and spring mattress factories. These new industries employed many city residents and served local, regional, and national markets.

Frederick expanded not only its economic base during this period. The number of homes constructed also grew, as some of the large plots of land on the city's fringes were developed. The new neighborhoods reflected late nineteenth-century architectural styles, as well as designs becoming popular with the advance of suburbanization. In some of these new developments, larger homes rested farther back from the curb, on tree-lined lawns and on lots more ample than the narrow lots laid out in Frederick's core during the Colonial era.

The first post–Civil War neighborhood was built along East Third Street, east of East Street. According to an 1873 map of Frederick, this area was part of a swath of land owned by the Jesuit Novitiate. By 1891, the street was extended and local businessman David Lowenstein subdivided the land and sold the lots. It was the first planned addition to Frederick since the initial lots were laid out in 1745 (lots were sold along Patrick Street west of Bentz Street soon after Frederick Town was developed, but the lots were irregularly shaped and sold individually). "So well has this enterprise succeeded," historian Williams wrote, "that now but little is left unimproved, and the taxable basis of the city has been much increased by the building up of this portion of the town."

Three years later, in 1894, Clarke Place was laid out, extending east from South Market Street and located south of the Maryland School for the Deaf. The neighborhood boasted a macadam-paved street, the latest innovation, and Norway maple trees planted in manicured lawns. Commercial development was not allowed. Three men, Willard C. Keller, Harry Bowers, and Dr. Alleine Williamson Sr. bought the land, and John Ramsburg laid out the lots. The street was named for General James C. Clarke, a Frederick native who was a president of the Chesapeake and Ohio Canal and president of the Illinois Central Railroad. Clarke donated a fountain that graced the public square in front of the courthouse.

Another residential development was laid out in western Frederick in 1905. Elihu Rockwell built a house across Bentz Street from the western end of Third Street in 1855, and lived there 28 years prior to his death in 1883. Frank C. Norwood bought the land from Rockwell's estate, extended Third through the property, and laid out Rockwell Terrace, named for the former resident. The new neighborhood offered a macadam street, concrete sidewalks, Norway maple trees, sanitary sewer, and water hookups. Restrictions were included in the lot deeds to protect the appearance of the homes and preserve the peace and character of the neighborhood. These rules required the houses to be designed in similar styles, prohibited commercial development, and forbade the sale or trade of "intoxicants" in the neighborhood. Williams called Rockwell Terrace "the finest portion of Frederick."

Other street extensions included East Church Street east of East, Market Street north of Eighth Street, and Fourth Street west of Bentz Street. The Fourth Street extension was named Dill Avenue for Lewis Dill, who owned property along the street.

Improvements to Frederick's infrastructure were completed to serve these new neighborhoods and the rest of the city. The telephone arrived in 1883. Electric street lights replaced gas lights beginning in 1887, and the following year the city erected a municipal electric plant with the capacity to light 76 lamps. In 1890, the Frederick Electric Light and Power Company built a $30,000 plant that provided light, power, and heat to the city's houses, stores, and manufacturing plants. In 1895, the city completed a second reservoir on the south side of West Seventh Street on the site of the present Max Kehne Memorial Park, which at that time was just west of the city limits. In the center of the reservoir was a fountain. In 1900, the city began repaving its cobblestone streets with bricks for smoother, quieter travel and slower wear and tear. East Church Street was the first to be repaved. When city officials saw the improvement, Market Street was also repaved, and the rest of the city followed soon afterward.

The Frederick County grand jury criticized the construction of the reservoir in its February 1894 report to the court:

> The recent expenditure of $28,000 by the officials of Frederick City in the construction of a new reservoir when sufficient water to fill the old one in time of need was what was required and <u>not secured</u> and which new construction does <u>not</u> hold water appears to have been so unnecessary, unwise and <u>prodigal</u> as to at least deserve the strongest censure.

Before beginning the project, the city should have sought a competent engineer's advice about the least expensive form of construction. Then it should have asked the state legislature for permission to borrow money if necessary, and put the project before a public vote. According to the grand jury, the city built the reservoir and then sought the legislature's permission to borrow money. "Reckless expenditures of public moneys should not be made with such defective results," the grand jury chided.

Despite improvements in Frederick's infrastructure, unsanitary conditions persisted in Frederick. These conditions might have contributed to a diphtheria epidemic that struck Frederick in August 1881 and persisted through at least 1886. During that period, the disease killed more than 300 people of all backgrounds and sections of the city, many of them children. In 1886, a damning, graphic report to the Health Board of Frederick County by Health Officer Franklin B. Smith M.D. harshly criticized the filthy conditions Smith believed contributed to the spread of the disease. He identified seven most likely contributors: the canning industry; hog pens, stables, and compost heaps; slaughter shops; privies and cesspools; tanneries; Carroll Creek; and streets, alleys, gutters, and sewers. Essentially, Smith targeted areas where organic waste was allowed to fester in the open air and incubate germs. Much of this material flowed unfiltered into the creek.

One particularly pungent example Smith cited was located at a corn canning factory:

> I find an area of at least 100 feet square covered to the depth of from three to ten feet with green corn cobs, tomato offal and the manure of from 80 to 150 horses and mules. All this lies fermenting and rotting in the hot sun. This mass is expected to equal, when the season is over, 2,000 four-horse wagon-loads of compost, or 4,000 tons of the same, all to be hauled through our streets, a mixture deleterious to the health and disagreeable to the sensibilities of a civilized community.

The factory cited probably was the one operated by Lewis McMurray. Apparently, McMurray resented the criticism but eventually cooperated with the disease-prevention efforts. A group of prominent citizens held a banquet in his honor shortly before he died, in an effort to show appreciation for his company's contribution to the city and to make amends for the heavy criticism he had received during the epidemic.

Six years later, in 1892, the Frederick County grand jury examined sanitary conditions in the city. Although the problems reported were nowhere near as disturbing, the grand jury's report labeled the municipal government "criminally neglectful of their duty in these matters." Elsewhere the report stated, "We find that the town has been a most deplorably unsanitary condition, and to a certain extent is still so, although efforts are now being made by the authorities to remedy the evils."

The unsanitary conditions identified in the report illustrate to contemporary readers how far public sanitation standards have advanced in the past century. For instance, at city hall the grand jury found a "closet in bad condition," probably a bathroom, and "a urinal flowing directly out into the public streets." The grand jury also took issue with hog pens "in improper condition" and located too close to the street. When police reported the problems, the authorities did nothing. Garbage collection was hampered by a neglectful contractor who went unchallenged. In a separate section of the report, the grand jury also found that the jail's sewer system did not adequately contain "foul gases and odors which are liable to produce sickness."

"These evils have been a constant menace to the health of the town," the report stated. The grand jury concluded its tirade on a hopeful note, stating that the county health board, formed by state law in 1886, recently had begun "a vigorous crusade against these nuisances."

In the same report, the grand jury also reported on its investigation into other impediments to the smooth functioning of the city. It found that several ordinances were violated consistently. In particular, dogs were allowed to roam the streets unmuzzled during the summer. Merchants blocked the sidewalks with displays of goods, the ordinance against which "has in particular been unblushingly violated, and no check put to it." Teams of horses remained hitched in one place on the streets for longer than two hours. The strident report stated that the ordinances forbidding these situations were enforced so rarely that they "have all been practically dead letters." The grand jury investigated more than just crime, and the reports of its investigations provide a glimpse into everyday life.

African Americans continued to build strong neighborhood communities after the Civil War, despite racism and segregation. Most people lived on the south and east sides of town, on West All Saints Street, South Bentz Street, East Street, and East Church Street, and several side streets. Some African Americans also lived in northern Frederick, on Fifth, Sixth, and Seventh Streets, as well as North Bentz Street, Middle Alley, and Maxwell Alley. Some African Americans were employed as servants for white families or in the city's hotels. They also held several other types of jobs, including tanner, mason, shoemaker, and farm laborer.

By the 1880s, blacks were losing some of the gains obtained immediately after the Civil War. The Supreme Court declared some post–Civil War civil rights legislation unconstitutional, and then, in the 1896 case of *Plessy v. Ferguson*, ruled that segregation of blacks into "separate but equal" facilities was legal. In reality, however, the facilities were not equal. In Frederick, this meant that blacks could shop at stores for food and other merchandise, but could not try on clothes or eat food purchased in the establishment on site. Some stores barred blacks altogether.

Blacks continued to build their own institutions in Frederick. Businesses offering a variety of services were located along West All Saints Street and included restaurants, groceries, clothing stores, and barber and beauty shops. African Americans ran the businesses that provided goods and services to black residents. According to the 1887 city directory, at least two butchers served the black community, J.M. Francis at 81 W. All Saints Street and Charles Mahoney on East Street between Church and Second

Streets. Three barbers were listed, one on East Fourth Street and two on West All Saints. Other black businesses listed in the city directory included two musicians, two groceries, both on West All Saints, and a restaurant operated by William Taylor at 8 West All Saints. African Americans from Frederick and outlying rural areas traveled to West All Saints to both shop and socialize.

One critical service regularly denied to African Americans by white medical facilities was medical care. Two black doctors rose to the challenge. In 1903, Dr. Ulysses Bourne established a medical practice in Frederick and served the community for 50 years. Blacks welcomed Dr. Bourne, who was the first black doctor in Frederick County, but whites did not. That did not stop him. He became the first president of the Maryland Negro Medical Association in 1940, helped charter the Frederick County chapter of the National Association for the Advancement of Colored People (NAACP), and was the first black person from western Maryland to run for the Maryland House of Delegates. With all his achievements, it is no wonder that Dr. Bourne was known as "the black mayor of Frederick." He died in 1956.

Another black doctor, Charles Brooks, also served Frederick's African Americans in his practice until 1936. Drs. Brooks and Bourne opened a hospital at an Elks lodge on West All Saints. The hospital served the medical needs of African Americans, who were not allowed admission to the local hospital, Frederick City Hospital. The black hospital operated until the late 1920s, when the city hospital opened a "colored" section in the hospital to serve blacks. Dr. George Joseph Snowball began meeting local dental needs in 1913. He practiced in Frederick for 57 years and retired in 1970 at the age of 92. He lived 13 more years, dying in 1984 at the age of 105.

Two other well-known African-American residents were artists. W.C. Bell was a photographer whose images documented, among other things, local women and children. William T. Grinage, a painter, is known for a 1917 painting of Jesus Christ and also for a 1923 painting of Francis Scott Key. The Frederick Kiwanis commissioned the painting and hung it in the Francis Scott Key Hotel on West Patrick Street.

Various African-American civic organizations rounded out daily life. The Pythian Castle was built in 1876 at 110 W. All Saints Street and housed Black Masonic Lodge No. 12. Its ladies' auxiliary was the first chartered in Maryland. The Emancipation Building at 158 W. All Saints Street, built to commemorate the 1863 Emancipation Proclamation, was used to house events. The *Afro-American Speaker*, a weekly newspaper, served African Americans in Frederick. The African American Female Unity Society of Frederick was organized in approximately 1900. The Young Men's Colored Reading Club met from 1913 to 1916. Each member read a book and met to hear each others' reports on their chosen books. A free "colored library" was organized in 1916 in the living room of 113 Ice Street and operated until the 1950s. Later organizations included a Boy Scout troop that formed in 1920, a kindergarten that began in 1937 in the Pythian Castle, and a semi-professional baseball team called the Richfield Eagles.

As the twentieth century dawned, new community institutions were organized to serve Frederick residents. Frederick City Hospital was chartered in 1898, and Emma

J. Smith donated 7 acres bordered by Park Avenue, Park Place, and Seventh Street for the building. In 1901, the cornerstone was laid in a ceremony featuring the Masons of Lynch Lodge 163 and the United Fire Company Drum and Bugle Corps. The two-story brick building was opened on May 1, 1902 with 16 private rooms and three wards. The hospital's first nursing class, consisting of four students, graduated in 1904. Hood College benefactor Margaret Scholl Hood donated money in 1905 for the Hood Wing on the south side of the hospital and for the James Mifflin Hood Wing on the north side in 1907. X-ray equipment was installed in 1912, a maternity ward and clinical lab were added in 1914, and a baby ward was added in 1916. The hospital was renamed Frederick Memorial Hospital in 1952 and has continued to add services and serve more patients.

The Young Men's Christian Association (YMCA) constructed a building in 1907 at the southeast corner of West Church and Court Streets. The YMCA was active in Frederick previously, but never owned its own building. The building was constructed for more than $60,000 after a fundraising campaign lasting about a year. Amenities included reading rooms stocked with newspapers and magazines, pool tables, two bowling alleys, a swimming pool, a gymnasium, and a banked running track. Living quarters for 22 men were located on the third floor, and were "fitted out with the best beds and mattresses, chiffoniers, chairs, electric lights and steam heat, and rent at rates that can be met by the young man of average income," according to Williams. Female members had access to the gym, swimming pool, bowling alleys, and a pool table once a week. A café faced Court Street. The building was demolished in the mid-1960s.

The Frederick County Chamber of Commerce was chartered in 1912. The organization was the first to be chartered by the U.S. Chamber of Commerce. The national organization formed after President William Howard Taft organized a national business conference, to which the Frederick Board of Trade was invited. The Frederick County Chamber of Commerce's first president was D. John Markey, who was a private in the Spanish-American War, an assistant football coach at Western Maryland College, and head coach at Maryland Agricultural College. In 1903 he took over his father's hat and glove store at 9 N. Market Street. He later ran for the U.S. Senate and the House of Representatives. The Frederick County Chamber of Commerce has represented the interests of county businesses for the past 91 years.

By the end of the nineteenth century, Frederick had long since recovered from the instability of the Civil War. It was now ready to face the highs and lows of the early twentieth century.

Chapter Six

HIGHS AND LOWS (1915-1945)

As the twentieth century advanced, a modernized Frederick faced the modern world. City infrastructure recently had been improved to the standards of the period, and modern innovations such as the auto and movie theaters made their appearance. However, Frederick's economic base struggled due to lack of industry. And, like the rest of the country, Frederick also was affected by national and international events, such as the influenza epidemic, the Great Depression, and two world wars. The first half of the twentieth century truly was a time of highs and lows.

By 1914, Frederick's population had grown to 14,000. Hitching posts were removed from Market and Patrick Streets a year earlier. The Frederick County Cooperative Extension Service agent's 1917 report predicted a bright future for Frederick and the larger county. "This is a very prosperous county. There are 22 banking institutions in the county with over $21,000,000 resources. In Frederick City alone there are seven banking institutions with over $1,000 on deposit for every inhabitant of the city."

In 1918, more farm work was available than there were laborers to do it. The Cooperative Extension Service agent reported that his advisory committee met with the Frederick City Board of Trade (later called the Chamber of Commerce) to find ways to address the labor shortage. The Board of Trade appointed a committee to canvas Frederick to recruit laborers. The effort netted 175 men, but only three requests for farm labor were received.

Minor league baseball had been a favorite pastime on sunny summer days for several years. Frederick first fielded a minor league team in 1907 or 1908, when the semi-professional Sunset League formed. The league lasted until 1911. Three years later, the semi-professional Tri-City League included teams from Frederick and Hagerstown, Maryland; and Martinsburg, West Virginia. The longest-lived league, the Blue Ridge League, began in 1915, according to a history of the league written by Mark Zeigler. It included Frederick and five other cities in the region. The Frederick Hustlers played their home games at the fairgrounds. Frederick took the league pennant during the first season. World War I, a flu epidemic, and shaky finances cancelled the 1919 season, but league play returned in 1920 and lasted until 1930 when the Blue Ridge League disbanded.

And then there were the lows. In 1917, the United States entered a world war that had been raging for three years. Frederick's men fought in Company A, 115th Infantry of the 29th Division, which was called the Blue and Gray Division because it included units from the north and the south. At home, residents supported the war effort by planting war gardens, buying war savings stamps, participating in fundraising campaigns of the Red

Cross, the YMCA, and other organizations, and increasing food production and conservation. Frederick County agricultural organizations canvassed the county to spread the word about the various local war-related activities and to hold patriotic meetings.

One effect of the war also touched civilians. An influenza epidemic swept the world during the war, partly spread by filthy living conditions on the front. Locally, as previous outbreaks of sickness had done, the influenza epidemic frightened Frederick residents, curtailed their activities, and took lives. The Frederick County fair was cancelled in 1918, just one of many local events cancelled during the epidemic to prevent the spread of the disease. The disease was to blame for half of American troop deaths in the war. It killed nearly 22 million people, or 1 percent of the world's population, and one-quarter of the U.S. population.

According to some historians, after the war, Frederick men returned to find few jobs other than farm work. No efforts were being made to attract industry. Longtime residents wanted the city to remain productive but quiet. Frederick County took up the largest land area in the state, but by 1920, Baltimore, Allegany, and Washington Counties were more populated. However, some industries were located in Frederick. The city's 1923 city directory listed The Frederick Iron & Steel Co., The Frederick Engineering Co., American Foundry & Manufacturing Co., and Ox Fibre Brush Co., among others. A 1927 promotional pamphlet boasted that the city hosted 43 manufacturing plants, including Union Manufacturing Co., which employed 250 people in the production of hosiery; Everedy Company, which manufactured bottle cappers, jelly strainers, syphon filters, and door closers since 1920; corn and tomato canning factories that made the city a national canning center; a flouring mill; and Frederick County Products Inc.

Yet Frederick retained its longtime status as a regional and national crossroads. The old turnpike between Baltimore and Frederick, which had become part of the old National Road to Illinois, received a new name. In 1926, the road was designated U.S. Route 40, including it in the new federal highway system of national auto routes enabling interstate auto travel. The arrival of train travel in the 1830s cut into the turnpike business, but with the growing popularity of the automobile and the improvement of highways, train travel declined and auto travel increased. Frederick was a stop on an interstate travel network, but no longer by teams of horses and stagecoach. This time, automobiles and other vehicles rumbled through town. Eleven years later, in 1937, passenger train service on the B&O Railroad from Frederick to Baltimore was terminated.

As it had in the nineteenth century, the road brought commerce to twentieth-century businesses in Frederick. Drivers stopped for refreshment at such establishments as the Francis Scott Key Hotel. The hotel opened in 1923 on the northeast corner of West Patrick and North Court Streets, the latest in a long line of hotels, inns, and taverns in Frederick and on the site. According to the 1927 Frederick promotional pamphlet, 7,000 cars passed by the hotel every day:

> Many of them, of course, stop at the Francis Scott Key Hotel up there on
> the corner, which was built by the people of the community a few years ago

at a cost of $1,050,000. Visitors are almost unanimous in declaring it the finest hotel they've seen in a town of his size; and they must like it, because its patrons number more than one hundred and eighty-six thousand annually, and it is doing a rapidly increasing volume of business, which now amounts to more than $320,000 a year.

Local residents also bought cars. The first auto dealers started selling cars in Frederick in the first years of the twentieth century. Within a few years, Frederick County began levying an automobile tax. These tax records illustrate the types of cars city residents bought and the price ranges. For instance, in December 1915, George T. Phebus paid $1,500 for his Cadillac, while Allen M. Pitzer's Ford cost $510. Holmes D. Baker, the son of Frederick philanthropist Joseph Dill Baker, owned two cars, a Buick and a Packard. Other models driven by Frederick residents included Saxon, Apperson, Maxwell, Studebaker, Hudson, and Overland.

The cultural and entertainment options available to Frederick residents continued to grow. The Civic Club established the first free library, the Frederick County Free Library, in 1914 at the YMCA building. Previously, in 1865, a group of men established a subscription library at Frederick College, at the northeast corner of Council and Record Streets, but the venture failed in 1870. In 1916 the free library moved to the Frederick College building, but by the mid-1920s the building no longer was adequate. It was demolished in 1936 and the C. Burr Artz Library was built. The library was named for Christian Burr Artz, a former Frederick resident whose wife, Margaret Thomas Artz, bequeathed part of her estate in 1887 to establish a library upon the death of her daughter, Victorine, as long as she did not marry. When Frederick residents learned of Mrs. Artz's will after her 1887 death, they began raising money, and thus the Civic Club was incorporated. Victorine indeed did not marry, and when she died in 1931 the library effort received $160,000. The library remained at this location from 1936 to 1982, when it moved to 110 E. Patrick Street.

The Tivoli Theater opened on December 23, 1926, one of the opulent movie palaces of the era, owned by the Stanley Cramer Company. Massive crystal chandeliers illuminated the auditorium, and patrons sat on plush velvet rocking chairs. Mosaic tile floors, satin brocade wall panels, and marble columns added to the ornate effect. A Wurlitzer pipe organ accompanied the first film shown, the silent film "The Strong Man." Construction cost $350,000.

The Tivoli was probably the most beautiful and most high-class theater in Frederick, but not the first. Frederick had been enjoying "moving pictures" since at least 1906. The Opera House was showing "The Edison Moving Pictures" that year, and the Bi Jou Family Theater was showing pictures in 1907. This theater, located on North Market Street, later became the Empire Theater. A short walk away on North Market was the Frederick Theater. It had earlier lives as the Marvel, Star, and the Maryland. As the Star, the theater was nicknamed "Mad House" because patrons reacted to performances by shouting and throwing soda bottles and candy boxes into the aisles. This theater showed mainly westerns, and it drew the most crowds.

Thanks to a local physician who had a fortuitous meeting with a movie studio executive in the 1930s, the Tivoli was Frederick's first air-conditioned public building. A Walkersville horseman named W.L. Brann invited Dr. Eddie Thomas to attend a prestigious California horse race, the Santa Anita handicap. At the event, Dr. Thomas met Jack Warner of Warner Brothers, which at that time owned the Tivoli. Dr. Thomas told Warner to bet on Brann's horse, Challedon, and Warner made a fortune. Warner wanted to repay Dr. Thomas, and the doctor, a regular patron of the Tivoli, knew just what to ask for. Warner paid the $100,000 cost of the 2-ton compressors built at the theater. On hot summer days, many people came to the Tivoli not only to enjoy a show but to escape the heat.

The theaters were segregated. Blacks were allowed into the Opera House but had to sit upstairs. The Frederick Theater allowed blacks, too, but at a side entrance. William O. Lee, an African American and a former Frederick alderman, recalled in the 1997 documentary *Up from the Meadows: A History of Black Americans in Frederick County, Maryland* that blacks were not allowed into the Tivoli at all. Lee said that his brother was light-skinned enough to slip in without being noticed. African-American audiences enjoyed a night at the movies at the Pythian Castle on West All Saints Street.

Radio, another addition to the cultural scene, came to Frederick at 2:30 p.m. on January 1, 1936. More than 400 people attended a luncheon at the Francis Scott Key Hotel to celebrate the inauguration of WFMD-AM. The first broadcast came from a studio in the hotel and included as speakers the city attorney, Edward J. Miller, speaking on behalf of Mayor Lloyd C. Culler, who could not attend; philanthropist Joseph D. Baker, who lived in a suite of rooms on the hotel's fifth floor; and state Senator Harry W. LeGore. Ten years later, in 1946, WFMD-FM began broadcasting, and later became WFRE-FM. For many years, WFMD broadcast from the former Groff Mansion at Seventh and Market Streets, built in the 1890s for Union Army Captain Joseph Groff and Susan Smith Groff, his wife. The building was demolished, despite efforts to preserve it.

Frederick residents built other community institutions during the 1920s and 1930s. Starting with Lincoln High School in 1923, several schools were built or established, some of which still are educating students today. Jewish residents, who had a history in Frederick of nearly 200 years, established their first house of worship in 1923. Baker Park was dedicated in 1927.

The greatest achievement of John W. Bruner, the supervisor of black schools in Frederick County, was to establish a high school for black students on West All Saints Street in 1920. Twenty-five students attended. Two years later, the Board of Education purchased 8 acres on West Madison Street, and in 1923 Lincoln High School opened. It was the only black high school in Frederick County for the next 35 years. In 1939, elementary school facilities were added after the consolidation of the black elementary schools in Frederick, West Seventh, and South Bentz. Lincoln's largest graduating class was the Class of 1958, which totaled 62 students. Even though Lincoln received fewer resources than the white schools, students had fond memories of their time at Lincoln, and dedicated teachers worked hard to educate their students. "We were taught by industrious, established, and well-educated black teachers who nurtured us with love and gave us hope, pride, integrity, and a sense of accomplishment," Joy Hall Onley wrote in *Dear Old Faithful Lincoln*. In 1962, Lincoln High School was transformed into South Frederick Elementary School, which served students regardless of race.

The white high schools in Frederick also underwent changes. Male and female high school students began attending school together in 1922, when Boys High School and Girls High School merged. The newly created Frederick High School began its first school year in fall 1922 at the Boys High School, constructed in 1912 at the northern head of Elm Street. The first principal of the new coeducational school was W.K. Klingaman, who previously was a teacher at a coed school in Bel Air. The Boys High School principal, G. Nevia Rebert, resigned to lead the Department of Education at Hood College. The new high school's vice principal was Charles H. Remsburg, principal of Girls High School. Although he only remained at the school for three years, Klingaman created an impression from the start. When Klingaman was coach of the Cadets basketball team during the 1924–1925 school year, the team won its first state championship.

Frederick High School moved to its current location on Carroll Parkway in 1940. The school was dedicated on May 31, 1940, and the Class of 1940 held its graduation ceremony in the school's auditorium, despite not having attended the school.

The oldest currently operating elementary school, Parkway Elementary School, opened in 1930. The school was built overlooking Baker Park, on the south side of Carroll Parkway between College Avenue and North Jefferson Street. The contractor for the construction was Lloyd C. Culler, who served seven terms as mayor and was a contractor and builder of several other public buildings in town. Culler Lake was dedicated in his honor in 1940.

The first synagogue in Frederick, Beth Sholom, was established in 1923. The institution, in the former Elks Lodge building at 20 W. Second Street, was six years in the making. In 1917, attorney Leo Weinberg encouraged Frederick Jews to make efforts to start a synagogue, but World War I intervened. After the war, in 1921, local Jewish women formed a local chapter of the National Council of Jewish Women and began working toward a permanent house of worship. At a meeting of the organization that year, Rabbi William Rosenau of Baltimore announced that Weinberg and his wife, Rae, would donate the Elks Lodge building in memory of Leo Weinberg's parents, Samuel and Amelia Lowenstein Weinberg, for a synagogue. The building was renovated, and a dedication ceremony was held on September 2, 1923. Rabbi Rosenau gave the dedication sermon. Dr. Menahem T. Friedman was elected rabbi of the synagogue.

In 1927, the city government's plans for a large municipal park along Carroll Creek on the west side of town became reality. The city had purchased several properties west of Bentz Street for the park, but still did not own two necessary properties, the old creamery and the Reifsnider property. Joseph Dill Baker and his wife bought the land and donated it to the city. On June 23, 1927, the city held a dedication ceremony for the new park. Nearly two months later, on August 12, the park's name was changed to Joseph Dill Baker Park, in honor of the man known as "Frederick's First Citizen." Baker was a prominent local businessman and philanthropist. Born in Buckeystown, he moved to Frederick as a young man and bought a tannery from John Loats. Among his other business ventures, Baker organized the Citizens National Bank in 1886 and was its first president. He was considered for Maryland governor in 1908. He saw to it that the city's cobblestone streets were paved, helped the YMCA construct its building at Church and Court Streets, donated funds to Frederick City Hospital to construct a wing for African-American patients, and donated land for Calvary United Methodist Church. Three years after his death, his friends arranged for a tower and carillon with bells to be constructed at the park. Ground was broken on April 2, 1941, and 14 bells were installed in the carillon on November 17. Later, a band shell was built.

Baker Park was not meant for African Americans. Lord Dunmore Nickens recalled in *Memories of Frederick . . . Over on the Other Side* that, when he was 19, he was arrested and fined $2.50 for trespassing on city property, simply for walking in the park. The all-black Owls softball club was supposed to play a white team at the park, but the police put a stop to it. A year after Baker Park was dedicated, Joseph Dill Baker donated land south of Carroll Creek between Court and Bentz Streets for a park for blacks. It was named Mullinix Park in honor of businessman Lorenzo Mullinix, who proposed the park. In 1948, when a swimming pool was built at Baker Park for white residents, Joseph Dill Baker's children Holmes Baker and Charlotte Markell Baker King donated funds for a pool at Mullinix Park. They stipulated that it be named for William Robert Diggs, an African-American employee of the Baker family for more than 50 years.

While they had built a solid, thriving community, African Americans still struggled with harsh race-based limits and discrimination. For instance, the Ku Klux Klan made its presence known in the 1920s during the trial of Charles Robinson, a black man accused of murdering a white woman. The trial was held at the Frederick County Courthouse. The Klan threatened to kidnap Robinson and hang him. The sheriff and his deputies kept the Klan at bay. Meanwhile, blacks and concerned whites came to Frederick from Baltimore and Washington, D.C. and spent the night, armed and standing sentry, on the roofs of buildings along South and All Saints Streets.

The Frederick County chapter of the National Association for the Advancement of Colored People was formed in June 1933. A year later, the organization sent a letter to the mayor and Board of Alderman requesting city services that seem basic today. The letter requested streetlights near Lincoln High School, regular garbage removal in all black neighborhoods, and better accommodations at Mullinix Park.

October 1929 marked the beginning of a significant low period in Frederick and the nation. The Great Depression reverberated through Frederick, damaging the economy and throwing people out of work. Frederick County's lack of industry prolonged the economic difficulties. The Central Trust Company, on the northeast corner of North Market and East Church Streets, closed in 1931. Many families never fully recovered their savings. President Franklin Roosevelt's New Deal programs, such as the Works Progress Administration, the Public Works Administration, and the Civilian Conservation Corps, provided jobs to unemployed men in Frederick and the larger county. Workers repaired roads and bridges, and built shelters and picnic facilities at state and county parks in the Frederick area, including Gambrill State Park and Yellow Springs Park.

The country was still shaking off the effects of the Depression in the late 1930s when war erupted in both Europe and Asia. World War II began in 1939 when Germany invaded Poland. Even though the United States remained neutral, the country prepared for war. In Frederick, Maryland National Guard units were mustered into federal service. The city and the American Legion post collaborated on a home defense plan. In 1940, a Frederick County draft board was formed, and men were drafted into military service. Discarded aluminum was collected in countywide programs. In 1941, Alton Bennett was appointed Director of Civilian Defense.

War preparations also occurred at Detrick Field, northwest of Frederick. The Civil Aeronautics Administration leased the field in fall 1940 for a pilot training facility and built a hangar and several barracks. The federal government first leased the 92-acre field, located between Fourth and Seventh Streets, in 1929 as an emergency landing field. The 104th Aero Squadron, 29th Division of the Maryland National Guard used the field for training every summer from 1931 to 1940, and the field was named for the squadron's flight surgeon, Dr. Frederick Louis Detrick. Part of the field previously was used for military purposes, as the former Camp Ordway of the District of Columbia National Guard. Another part of the field formerly was the adjacent D. Columbus Kemp farm.

When the Japanese attacked Pearl Harbor on December 7, 1941, many local men enlisted immediately or were drafted into all units of military service, and fought in the European and Asian theaters of war. Women packaged bandages for the Red Cross, and some residents worked in defense industries in Baltimore and Hagerstown. Students, too, participated in the war effort by forming Victory Corps that organized such projects as newspaper collections. The 104th Aero Squadron, which trained at Detrick Field, conducted anti-submarine patrols along the Atlantic coast in 1942. The last aircraft squadron based at Detrick Field, the 2nd Bombardment Squadron of the U.S. Army Air Corps, was deployed to England. Company A of the 115th Infantry, which had given distinguished service in World War I, was one of the first units to land on the beaches of Normandy in 1944.

The war disrupted life for civilians, too, according to writer and Frederick native Frances A. Randall, writing in the July 20, 2003 *Frederick News-Post*. A community rationing board monitored and restricted supplies of sugar, meat, tires, gasoline, coffee, fuel oil, and leather boots. Sales of new cars stopped, and the annual county fair was cancelled. Industries shifted their energies to war-related production. There were air raid drills, and most buildings had "blackout curtains" to block light in the event of an air raid.

Detrick Field became more than just a pilot training facility. The government bought the land in 1943, and on April 12 it became a temporary installation called Camp Detrick, under the command of the U.S. Army Chemical Warfare Service. The U.S. Biological Laboratories were established in 1943 at Camp Detrick. "The team of early scientists achieved pioneering efforts in decontamination, gaseous sterilization, and agent purification," according to a 1995 historical summary of Fort Detrick. Top-secret biological warfare research already had been conducted since 1941, research that Frederick residents were not fully aware of until after the war. This mission brought military personnel and scientists to the encampment. Some needed housing in Frederick, and many came into the city to socialize at the USO at the All Saints Church parish hall. After the war, Camp Detrick's mission was to conduct biological research and development, specifically to develop vaccines to defend against chemical and biological attacks and to find ways to respond to a biological weapons attack. Camp Detrick was renamed Fort Detrick and made a permanent installation in 1956.

General optimism that had been gone since 1941 returned with the victories of V-E Day in April 1945 and V-J Day in August. The optimism remained after the war. Postwar prosperity promised to bring economic development and growth to Frederick, but also changes that transformed Frederick in positive and negative ways.

Chapter Seven

POSTWAR PROSPERITY (1945–1970s)

Unlike after previous wars, World War II veterans returning home to Frederick had promising prospects. In the postwar period, industries in Frederick County were expanding and new industries were moving here. Camp Detrick was designated a permanent installation. Houses were under construction, and highway improvements gave Frederick residents more mobility and shortened travel times to Hagerstown, Baltimore, and Washington, D.C. New shopping centers expanded the tax base. New schools served the growing population. These changes benefited Frederick, but also brought new challenges, such as congestion and threats to the economic vitality of downtown.

Frederick received federal and state funds in 1944 to buy land north of East Patrick Street for a municipal airport. At that time, the land was located east of the city. The first plane landed at the airport on April 17, 1946, while the facility was still under construction. The airport was completed three years later and was dedicated May 1, 1949. The terminal building was named after William Theodore Delaplaine III, the first Frederick pilot to die in World War II. He died in 1943, in a crash of a twin engine navy transport plane near Oakland, California. The airport began by offering passenger and air cargo service, and today Frederick Municipal Airport is one of the East Coast's busy small airports. It is a reliever airport for the region's major airports: Baltimore-Washington International, Reagan National, and Dulles. More than 300 businesses use the airport annually, and it is the base for one of eight Maryland State Police MEDEVAC units.

The federal government made Camp Detrick a permanent installation on February 1, 1956. Present-day Fort Detrick encompasses approximately 1,200 acres. The 800-acre main post is called Area A. Area B, part of the former Krantz property on Shookstown Road, is a testing area of 398 acres that the government bought in 1946. One element of the installation's research facilities was a 40-foot diameter, steel-plated, spherical chemical testing facility called the "eight ball." It was built in 1950 and used until 1969, during which time it was the largest of its kind in the world. The sphere was listed in the National Register of Historic Places in 1977 for its contributions to science. Another research facility was the seven-story Building 470, in which scientists cultured anthrax and other agents in the 1950s.

The installation continued to employ hundreds of people who boosted the population and the economy of the city and the county. Frederick's population grew to 24,000 in the 1950s, partly because of the influx of Fort Detrick employees. However, in November 1969, President Richard M. Nixon signed an executive order outlawing offensive biological research, potentially damaging the local economy. The jobs of more than 1,000 Frederick residents would be eliminated. The city's population dropped to 23,641 in 1970, partly because of this ban on biological research.

Fortunes turned in Frederick's favor nearly two years later, however. A crowd of 2,000 gathered at Fort Detrick to hear President Nixon announce that the research facilities would be mustered into the battle against a different enemy, cancer. In the mid-1990s, the Frederick Cancer Research and Development Center consisted of 67 buildings on approximately 70 acres, and it employed 2,000 people. Besides conducting cancer research, scientists also research AIDS and other infectious diseases, develop medical equipment, and conduct genetic engineering. Fort Detrick also hosts defense communications facilities. Since 1959, the East Coast Telecommunications Center, one of 17 strategically located centers around the world, has relayed messages between the military, other government agencies, and the North Atlantic Treaty Organization. In 1978, when the "hotline" between the Kremlin and the White House was switched to satellite, Fort Detrick's antennas were linked by satellite with Soviet antennas to ensure that the American and Soviet heads of state were immediately accessible to each other.

As Frederick's population continued to grow in the 1950s, more schools were needed at all educational levels. Several additional schools operating today began serving Frederick students. North Frederick Elementary School, located at 1001 Motter Avenue, was built in 1954 to serve families who were moving into the new postwar neighborhoods sprouting north of downtown. Frederick Community College held its first classes in 1957, in the evening at Frederick High School. The community college was located in the former elementary and high school building at 520 N. Market Street in 1966. It moved to its own campus on Opossumtown Pike, on the north end of the city, in 1971. West Frederick Middle School opened in 1958 at 515 W. Patrick Street. South Frederick Elementary School opened in 1962, converted from the former Lincoln School, which served black students until Frederick County public schools were racially integrated. A second high school opened in Frederick in 1966, when Governor Thomas Johnson High School was built at 1501 N. Market Street.

Frederick's retail base expanded in the 1950s and 1960s, but the expansion's focus was not based in the city's downtown core. The additional retail businesses benefited the city's economy but threatened downtown Frederick's economic vitality. The city's first shopping center, Frederick Shopping Center, opened on West Seventh Street northwest of downtown in 1957. Its concentration of stores and ample parking attracted customers who were part of an increasingly auto-centered culture. Woolworth's left downtown and relocated there. The shopping center later included smaller businesses and a grocery store. The growth of the "Golden Mile" retail corridor on Route 40 west of downtown and the Francis Scott Key Mall along Buckeystown Pike south of Frederick sapped more retail dollars from downtown. JC Penney and Montgomery Ward left downtown and relocated to Fredericktowne Mall, which opened on the Golden Mile in 1972. As most small and mid-sized cities did, Frederick's downtown was changing because large businesses were leaving and taking their customers with them.

However, city officials already had begun to realize the historical, aesthetic, and commercial value of preserving historic structures downtown. In April 1952, Mayor Donald B. Rice appointed a historic zone committee to survey Frederick and determine which buildings needed to be preserved. In a report completed after the survey, the committee recommended passage of an ordinance designating historic areas and requiring an architecture commission to review requests for alteration, reconstruction, or demolition of structures in the district.

"We have got to learn to exploit our historical sites," Charles F. Bowers, an architect and former president of the Chamber of Commerce and the Historical Society of Frederick County, stated in the April 18, 1952 Baltimore *Sun*. "Maryland, and Frederick, too, has really missed the boat when it comes to attracting tourists. We get them here to see the Barbara Fritchie house, but that is all."

In the 1960s, the Maryland General Assembly gave municipalities the authority to create historic district commissions with regulatory authority. In January 1968, seven city residents were appointed to Frederick's first such historic district commission. Its first order of business was to create a master plan identifying improvements needed in the district and alteration restrictions to be imposed. The creation of the commission came none too soon for Richard Lebherz, writing in the February 5, 1968 *Frederick Post*. "A few years back some rather hideous-looking facades went up over the fronts of old buildings on Market Street. Instead of enhancing downtown Frederick, they made it look more like a slum area. Even the word 'ghastly' doesn't do for a description."

Lebherz said shop owners would benefit financially if they cooperated with the commission. "If there is any resistance on the part of the shopkeeper or owner to go along with these ideas, perhaps it might be a good thing for him to realize that if these historic preservations are made, they will lure tourists into Frederick again, not around it." A historic district was established, and it was listed on the National Register of Historic Places in 1973.

Frederick's transportation infrastructure changed to accommodate the shift in travel from train to auto. Trolley service on the Hagerstown and Frederick Railway stopped in 1937, but was revived in World War II when the cars were used to haul salvaged material from Jefferson Street to Camp Detrick. The last trolley traveled to Middletown in 1947. The last train traveled to Thurmont in 1954, and in 1955 the electric lines were removed and diesel trains were used for freight service. The track between Fort Detrick and Thurmont was removed in 1958, but service continued to the East Street industrial areas. All service stopped on April 26, 1961.

The last passenger train traveled the Pennsylvania Railroad line in 1948, and freight trains stopped running in 1972, when Hurricane Agnes destroyed the railroad line over the Monocacy River Bridge. By 1977, the station on East Street between Patrick and Church Streets was razed to make room for the post office and its loading areas. Some tracks are still located on East, in the middle of the roadbed. Passenger service on the Baltimore and Ohio Railroad line to Washington, D.C. stopped in 1949; service to Baltimore had stopped in 1937.

Postwar Prosperity

By 1961, no passenger trains or trolleys served Frederick. Meanwhile, three highways had been constructed to link the city by automobile to Baltimore and Washington. Route 15 traveled north and south through western Frederick in the 1950s. The first section of what would be designated Interstate 270 was opened on January 27, 1953. It reached Clarksburg, north of Gaithersburg, in approximately 1964. In 1956, U.S. Route 40 still traveled through downtown Frederick on Patrick Street, but by 1963, it bypassed Frederick to the south as a freeway called the Baltimore National Pike. Patrick Street was designated the Old National Pike. As part of President Dwight D. Eisenhower's interstate highway system created in 1956, Interstate 70 was built in the 1960s. It followed the same path as Route 40, as a southern bypass of Frederick. In 1986 the road was improved to meet interstate standards. Patrick Street was designated Maryland Route 144. Changes to roads and traffic patterns also occurred in Frederick. Work began to extend East Street north of Eighth Street in 1953. The same year, a system of alternating one-way streets was put in place downtown to facilitate traffic flow.

The highways helped move the increasing traffic more quickly through the region, but they bypassed downtown, taking customers with them. One casualty was Francis Scott Key Hotel, on the northeast corner of West Patrick and North Court Streets. The hotel's popularity declined because travelers favored hotels on the outskirts of town. Loyola Federal Savings and Loan bought the hotel in 1965 and converted the old main dining room into a branch bank. In 1972, former Frederick County steel executive Norman W. Todd bought the hotel and extensively renovated it, but the slow economy kept travelers away. When Todd could not pay the $20,000 electric bill, Potomac Edison turned off the power on July 7, 1975, suddenly evicting guests, throwing 56 employees out of work, and forcing several community groups to find other meeting space. On July 9, the *Frederick News* editorialized that the closing was a "big blow for Frederick." The mortgage holder, Farmers & Mechanics National Bank sold the hotel at auction, and Homewood Retirement Centers of Williamsport, Maryland bought the building on September 3 for $360,000. Homewood opened a home care facility and nursing home in 1977.

Frederick residents participated in the social change and upheaval occurring in the 1950s and 1960s, although changes occurred at a calmer pace in Frederick than in other areas of the country. Racial integration was the most significant change. The U.S. Supreme Court ruled on May 17, 1954 that separate school systems were unequal. Two years later, in August 1956, Frederick County Public Schools officials announced that they would form a countywide school desegregation program. Based on the recollections of those who attended segregated schools, it is clear that the separate systems were not equal. William O. Lee, the former Frederick city alderman and longtime educator, recalled some of the disparities at Lincoln School in the May 25, 2003 *Frederick News-Post*. The science department had two old microscopes, sports equipment was "beat up," and the books were used. The white schools had used these materials and then handed them down to the black school when they no longer needed them. Also according to the article, Lincoln High School Principal Charles E. Henson was paid about half of what the white school principals made.

FREDERICK

The Board of Education approved the desegregation program in spring 1957, and it was implemented when students came back to school in the fall. That year, 15 black students attended Frederick High School. Lincoln, which also had an elementary section, closed after the 1961–1962 school year. According to Lee, school integration proceeded so smoothly in Frederick that a national magazine wrote about it.

Soon, more jobs were open to African Americans, especially after President Lyndon Johnson signed the 1964 Civil Rights Act prohibiting discrimination in facilities and employment. Irene Lee was the first black clerk to work in a white-owned store, Haber women's apparel store in Frederick Shopping Center. Blacks began to work in other stores and businesses. Previously, a few jobs were available in these places, but not the jobs in which African Americans would be visible to the public. Elected and appointed positions in city and county government also became available. George Fredericks was the first black person appointed to a titled county job, as Frederick County dogcatcher in 1965. Claude Delauter Jr. was the first African American elected to the Frederick city Board of Aldermen, in 1974.

But change did not take place to the extent and with the speed that African Americans wanted. On January 2, 1969, the Frederick Alliance of Businessmen met with local black leaders, including the Frederick chapter of the National Association for the Advancement of Colored People, in an effort to improve relations between the two groups. The black participants immediately identified basic problems that contributed to blacks' negative attitudes toward businesses. Business owners needed to require their employees to treat black customers with basic human respect, and needed to treat their black and white employees equally by eliminating separate dressing rooms and water fountains. They also criticized housing discrimination and a lack of white patronage of black businesses.

Black and white leaders in Frederick worked together to ensure order was maintained in the city as race-related civil unrest swept the country during this period. Lee recalled in the documentary *Up from the Meadows* that "dialogue groups" of blacks and whites met on Sundays to discuss concerns, and African Americans also met with city police officers. "Things were fairly quiet here," Lee recalled. A few incidents did occur, but not with regularity. Some young people threw rocks when George Wallace, a segregationist, former Alabama governor, and at the time a Presidential candidate, held a meeting at the Armory in 1972. That was the extent of the disturbance. "We kept things quiet. We kept the community down. We kept people at ease," Lee said.

Postwar prosperity, population and economic growth, and changing social attitudes enriched Frederick. However, some of these changes brought new challenges. Frederick residents and community leaders would need to find innovative and creative solutions to ensure that Frederick would continue to thrive.

Chapter Eight

FROM SETTLEMENT TO CITY

(1970s-2003)

On October 9, 1976, after an already rainy summer, a deluge hit Frederick. The storm brought not only plenty of water but also damage and destruction, all unwelcome arrivals in downtown Frederick.

After more than a week of steady rain, water started to overflow the banks of Carroll Creek. By late morning, the water had flooded basements and inundated first floors, trapping people in their homes. Cars were carried away, and South Market Street was passable only by boat. At the landmark Tivoli Theater, water submerged the seats and floated the Wurlitzer organ to the stage. No deaths occurred, but some people were injured, and those forced out of their homes were placed in temporary shelter at the Maryland School for the Deaf. Power, telephone, and water service was knocked out. President Gerald Ford declared the city a disaster area, and Frederick received $5 million in disaster relief funds. However, Frederick needed $25 million to repair all the damage, as few homeowners or businesses carried flood insurance. Many damaged buildings along South Market Street were condemned, and some businesses closed permanently.

Carroll Creek was to be cleaned and widened before the flood, but its devastation inspired calls for a more comprehensive way to prevent flooding. Long-term flood control also was needed to remove downtown Frederick from the floodplain so that new construction and economic development could occur, because federal regulations do not allow building in a floodplain. Frederick Mayor Ronald N. Young made completion of the project his personal goal upon taking office in 1973. In the resulting $60 million project, begun in 1985 and completed in 1996, 1.3 miles of concrete conduits were installed in the creek bed from Baker Park east to Highland Street. The conduits carry floodwater to the Monocacy River. The conduit project not only controls flooding, but also created space for an attractive linear park that hosts the annual Frederick Festival of the Arts.

The flood control project symbolized the story of Frederick from the late 1970s to today. Reuse and redevelopment helped Frederick transform itself to serve the needs of residents of the twenty-first century. Residential and commercial growth continued, although visions of development along the creek have not yet been realized. Frederick remains the second largest incorporated city in Maryland, but it still maintains the atmosphere of a relatively small town in a rural county.

FREDERICK

Before the flood, downtown Frederick property owners already had started banding together to improve the area. The Frederick Improvement Foundation formed to encourage these efforts. Owners made improvements to their properties, and the city placed overhead utilities underground, installed new streetlights, and planted trees. The floodwaters interfered with these efforts, and everyone started over again.

The flood inspired more substantial transformations. On February 9, 1978, the old Tivoli Theater reopened as the Weinberg Center for the Performing Arts. The flood could have doomed the building. The theater's popularity had declined in the 1950s and 1960s because of television and the new suburban multiplex theaters. By the mid-1970s the Tivoli was showing mostly X-rated films. After the flood, demolishing the building was considered. Instead, local individuals and companies donated their time and services to restore the grand old theater, at a cost of $175,000. The Weinberg Center was named for the Weinberg family, who by the 1970s owned the theater and donated it to the City of Frederick. The Weinberg regularly attracts audiences to its performances of nationally known musical artists, plays, and classic films.

The Weinberg Center was the first of several infusions of the arts into the city at the time. The Delaplaine Visual Arts Education Center opened in 1993 in the former Mountain City Mill on South Carroll Street just south of Carroll Creek. The building was named for the Delaplaine family, who with the Randall family donated the building to the city. Meanwhile, artist William Cochran painted several trompe l'oeil murals in downtown Frederick, known as the "Angels in the Architecture" series. Cochran's work also enhances the Carroll Street bridge over Carroll Creek. These arts endeavors are the latest in a long history of the arts in Frederick. Florence Doub, the first head of the Woman's College art department, started the Frederick Art Club in the late 1800s, and it was still going strong a century later. Through the years, local artists have maintained small galleries and studios. One longtime local artist was Helen Smith, who painted throughout the twentieth century until her death in 1997. William T. Grinage's 1923 painting of Francis Scott Key graced the Francis Scott Key Hotel on West Patrick Street.

One societal transformation had the potential to bring more business to downtown Frederick, but also forced some reluctant business owners to open on Sundays. Before 1987, under the "blue law," most Frederick County retail businesses were not allowed to open on Sundays. The law had colonial roots and was originally intended to reserve the day for Christians to attend church. The blue laws differed in each Maryland county. In the 1970s, some Frederick residents and business owners took issue with the law and wanted it repealed. The Frederick County Chamber of Commerce polled its members in 1977 and found that of 85 respondents, a majority supported retaining the laws, but that a substantial minority of 37 wanted to abolish them, according to the December 30, 1977 *Frederick News-Post*.

On the Sunday after Thanksgiving in 1979, Hess' Department Store in Francis Scott Key Mall pushed the issue by opening for business. The store was cited for violating the law, and three employees were served with criminal summonses. The Retail Committee of the chamber of commerce voted the following Thursday to support the blue laws and the sheriff's office in its enforcement of them. Chamber President William F. Ruehl told the *News-Post* that he was angry that Hess' chose to break the law during a lucrative weekend while other businesses obeyed the law by remaining closed. "It is a feeling in Frederick that you do not dip into someone else's pocket," Ruehl said, "and Hess' broke the law when it was most beneficial to them."

Ruehl said that a repeal of the blue laws would disrupt families. "I think the community deteriorates when the mother is forced to work when the children are home." He conceded that a family shopping excursion on a Sunday would make "a good family outing." Hess' vice president, Fred Bentelspacher, responded that a silent majority of Frederick County residents wanted to shop on Sundays. "Our surveys have shown that and our customers keep asking us to open on Sundays," he told the *News-Post*.

Hess' did not open the next Sunday, but the controversy did not diminish. Most of the approximately 50 people who attended the Frederick County state legislative delegation's annual public hearing aired their views on the issue. Blue law supporters consisted mostly of small downtown businessmen who believed that repealing the law would increase overhead costs. Opponents said Frederick County was losing Sunday business to Montgomery and other surrounding counties that did not have blue laws. The issue had not died a year later, when the Chamber of Commerce released a statement supporting the blue law but also called for a referendum in which voters would decide whether businesses could choose to remain open on Sundays between Thanksgiving and the Sunday after New Year's Day.

The *News-Post* encouraged elected officials to put the matter to a public vote, while one local merchant wrote a long letter describing his strenuous objections to repealing the blue law. "Do you really want to see Frederick become another Montgomery County?" wrote Michael D. Jones, owner of Chanticleer Shoes. "Do you want that 'rat race' way of life? LET'S KEEP FREDERICK FAR FROM THE MADDENING CROWD!"

This point of view did not prevail, and the blue law was repealed in 1987. Residents of the city and Frederick County shopped for the first time on a Sunday on July 5 of that year. Despite the previous controversy, there was no uproar, but plenty of fanfare, according to the June 30 *Frederick News-Post*. "Elaborate promotional plans—complete with clowns, giveaways, and hot air balloons—have been drawn up by management at the Francis Scott Key Mall and Frederick Towne Mall and other large retail outlets, in an effort to attract consumers to the first day of large-scale Sunday shopping in Frederick." Small merchants downtown, however, adopted a more low-key attitude. "Dick Kessler, owner of King's Men's Wear on South Market Street, said he has been firmly behind blue law repeal as a member of the Frederick County Chamber of Commerce, but will not open his store on Sundays—at least not yet. 'Maybe I'm wrong for not being one of the leaders in this,' he said, 'but personally, I want to be with my family on my day off.' "

In 1982, a transformation 15 years in the making was completed when construction of the Frederick County Courthouse was completed at the southwest corner of Patrick and Court Streets. The county's legal business had been conducted at the building on courthouse square since 1862, but the building had become too small. Chief Judge Robert E. Clapp Jr. asked the Frederick County grand jury in 1967 to investigate whether a new courthouse was needed. The site was selected in 1975, and ground was broken and a construction contract signed with CAM Construction Company in November 1978. Business at the court's new home began on July 26, 1982. Meanwhile, county commissioners had a historic courthouse on their hands that they no longer needed. The City of Frederick, which had been headquartered in the 100 block of North Market Street for more than 100 years, jumped at the chance to relocate. After two appraisals and negotiations between the city and the county, Frederick County commissioners voted on August 11 to sell the courthouse to the city for $500,000. The mayor and Board of Aldermen approved the purchase the same day, and a deed was signed on October 24, 1983. The city renovated the building for nearly $2 million.

On Frederick's south side, a stadium was built in 1990 to serve as the home of a Class A baseball team. The Frederick Keys, the Carolina League Class A affiliate of the Baltimore Orioles, had moved to Frederick in 1989 from Williamsport, Pennsylvania, and played its first season at McCurdy Field near Jefferson Street. Mr. and Mrs. M.J. Grove donated $250,000 toward the construction of a stadium on South Market Street. The stadium was named for Mr. Grove's father, James Henry "Harry" Grove, who was involved with the Frederick Hustlers until he died in 1930. The stadium has seating for 5,200 people, as well as 12 skyboxes and a restaurant and clubhouse. Many fans regularly come to the game on a warm summer afternoon or evening to watch the Keys play. A few famous visitors have attended games, including President George Bush in 1991 and 1992, and Attorney General John Ashcroft in 2002.

Passenger train service between Frederick and Washington, D.C. resumed on December 17, 2001, after a 52-year absence, when the MARC Brunswick line began serving Frederick. On that day, a conductor named "Captain Bly," the son of a crewman who operated the last Baltimore & Ohio trains, collected passenger tickets. Passengers catch the train at two stations in the area, the downtown Frederick station and the Monocacy station south of Frederick east of Urbana Pike. The train follows the old Metropolitan Railroad Company/Baltimore and Ohio Railroad line from Washington, D.C. to Point of Rocks, and then the B&O connection north to Frederick. The resumption of train service made it easier for commuters to move to Frederick. Another transportation improvement pursued in connection with the construction of the train station was the extension of East Street south of Patrick to South Street, its current ending point. The next phase of the project will be to extend East south to Interstate 70.

In May 2002, an expanded C. Burr Artz Library on East Patrick Street greeted patrons. The original building constructed at that location in 1982 cost $2.7 million, while the recent expansion cost nearly $11 million. An important part of the library's design was its orientation. The building's west side entrance preserves access to both Patrick Street and Carroll Creek. Library Director Darrell Batson also placed a premium on providing a visually pleasing interior and exterior. "I think a modern library should be a visual experience," he said in a pamphlet produced for the expanded building's grand opening. "The moment you walk into this library you should be learning. . . . There should be art on the walls and music in the air. We have comfortable furniture and tables. You see, we can compete with Borders and the arcades."

From Settlement to City

Women achieved several important leadership positions during this period. Elizabeth Burket, elected in 1973, was the first female alderman in Frederick. Dr. Martha Church became the first female president of Hood College in 1975 and served 20 years. Jennifer Dougherty took office in 2001 as Frederick's first female mayor, after first beating two candidates in the Democratic primary, including another female candidate, Alderman Meta Nash.

Redevelopment, reuse, and expansion continue in 2003. In March, Frederick was awarded a $16 million grant from the federal Department of Housing and Urban Development toward the demolition of two public housing developments, the John Hanson and Taney apartments, and the construction of mixed-income housing to replace them. The grant was awarded in HUD's HOPE VI program, which stands for Homeownership and Opportunity for People Everywhere. The Francis Scott Key Hotel, which opened in 1923 and was the Homewood retirement residence from 1977 to 2000, was transformed into luxury apartments with ground-level businesses. By 2003, all commercial space was leased.

In August, Frederick became the first Maryland municipality to receive a grant from the Environmental Protection Agency to assess environmental contamination levels in "brownfields," or vacant industrial lots, along Carroll Creek, according to *The Washington Post*. Frederick received $200,000 to test four lots. Once contamination levels are assessed, the city hopes to clean up the lots and sell them to developers. The city owns a total of 11 sites totaling more than 20 acres. Investors are considering construction and renovation projects along Carroll Creek, as evidenced by several announcements in local newspapers this year. Fort Detrick officials want to pursue a public-private partnership to construct a 400-room hotel and convention center just outside the installation.

Frederick is no longer an agricultural center to which farmers bring their produce to sell at the town hall market or to transport to larger cities via the railroad. Still, even in the twenty-first century, Frederick maintains a close connection to agriculture. Several businesses on Frederick's outskirts sell farm equipment and supplies. The Great Frederick Fair, with its rides, farm exhibits, and entertainment, continues to attract crowds every fall at the fairgrounds on East Patrick Street. Local farmers sell their produce at farmers markets at various locations in Frederick from spring through fall. And, as recently as August 2003, one family in southern Frederick kept eight chickens as family pets. According to a story in the August 30, 2003 *Frederick News-Post* that was ominously headlined, "Chickens evicted," city code enforcement inspectors required the family to get rid of the chickens.

In many ways, Frederick in 2003 is an entirely different city compared to its beginnings in 1745 as Frederick Town. First, even though it retains its historic status as one of the state's largest incorporated cities, Frederick today is much larger than ancestral Frederick Town. According to the 2000 federal census, Frederick's population of 52,767 ranked second in the state, next to Baltimore. Frederick's 2000 population represented an 87 percent increase over its 1980 population of 28,086. Frederick Town's first residents worshiped at Episcopal, Lutheran, and Reformed churches. Today, there are not only many more houses of worship, but also many more religious faiths.

FREDERICK

Educational opportunities were sparse in early Frederick, while today's Frederick students attend several elementary and middle schools and two high schools. New housing developments on the north and west sides of Frederick attract more residents. Antiques shops, boutiques, and restaurants provide an enjoyable night on the town for local residents or round out a weekend for out-of-town visitors touring city and county historical sites.

Nevertheless, Frederick residents still yearn to preserve rural atmosphere and open space. Those amenities are what drew many residents to move from more crowded areas of the region. Fredericktonians today hope that growth and open space can coexist. An editorial in the July 15, 2003 *Frederick News-Post* summed up this point of view when it opined on the closure of the state's Smart Growth office. The editorial encouraged state officials to allow westward growth to continue, but not without prudent planning. The editorial praised the commercial growth along Interstate 270 toward Frederick, but expressed the hope that the rural areas along Interstate 70 would grow more slowly:

> We're expecting more growth. We've watched Frederick Countians elect no-growth and slow-growth and careful-growth candidates for decades. We've heard the same refrain in Montgomery County and nearby Carroll County. But it just keeps coming. It's like the Incredible Hulk—sometimes you just have to get out of his way.
>
> But we're counting on the Maryland Department of Planning to offer good advice and oversight, which the old Smart Growth office had done, to allow those of us who live in Maryland and drive Maryland roads to have some semblance of normalcy and calmness.

That is essentially the story of Frederick history. From Frederick's beginnings, residents have tried to build a thriving and successful center of commerce, but also have fought to maintain the city's small-town charm. Over the past 258 years, Frederick continually has aimed to respond to changing times to ensure that both needs have gotten met. The city does not seem to be worse for wear as a result. In fact, as Frederick's many historic structures show, the city has held up nicely. After 258 years, it is clear that Daniel Dulany's land speculation paid off beyond his wildest dreams.

BIBLIOGRAPHY

Arnett, Earl, Robert J. Brugger, and Edward C. Papenfuse. *Maryland: A New Guide to the Old Line State*. Baltimore, MD: The Johns Hopkins University Press, 1999.

Asbury United Methodist Church. *165th Anniversary 1818–1983, Sunday May 8, 1983 thru Sunday May 15, 1983, Asbury United Methodist Church, All Saints and Court Streets, Frederick, Maryland*. Frederick: Asbury United Methodist Church, 1983.

Ashbury, John W. *. . . and All Our Yesterdays: A Chronicle of Frederick County, Maryland*. Frederick: Diversions Publications, 1997.

Axelrod, Alan. *The Complete Idiot's Guide to American History*. New York: Alpha Books, 1996.

"Blue law referendum." *Frederick Post*. 10 December 1980: Sec. A-6.

Burt, Charles R. *220 Years of Growing, Caring and Sharing 1770–1990, A History of Calvary United Methodist Church*. Frederick: Calvary United Methodist Church, 1990.

C. Burr Artz Library, Maryland Room. Frederick: vertical files.

Cannon, Timothy L., Tom Gorsline, and Nancy F. Whitmore. *Pictorial History of Frederick, Maryland: the First 250 years 1745–1995*. Frederick: Key Publishing Group, 1995.

City of Frederick. "Frederick Airport." www.cityoffrederick.com/departments/Airport/Main.htm

Commercial State Bank. *Let's Look Around Us at the New and Greater Frederick Development before Our Eyes*. Frederick: Commercial State Bank, 1927.

Covert, Norman M. *Cutting Edge: A History of Fort Detrick, Maryland 1943–1993*. Fort Detrick, MD: Public Affairs Office, 1993.

"The Delaplaine Visual Arts Education Center." www.delaplaine.org/about.html.

Diversions Publications. *Frederick County's 250th Commemorative*. Frederick: Diversions Publications, 1997.

Engelbrecht, Jacob. *The Diary of Jacob Engelbrecht*. Frederick: Historical Society of Frederick County, 2001.

Fields, Barbara Jeanne. *Slavery and Freedom on the Middle Ground*. New Haven, CT: Yale University, 1985.

Gordon, Paul P. "Was rebellion's start a conspiracy?" *The Gazette*. 5 December 2002: Sec. A-14.

Gordon, Paul P. and Rita S. *The Jews beneath the Clustered Spires*. Hagerstown, MD: Hagerstown Bookbinding and Printing Co., 1971.

———. *A Textbook History of Frederick County*. Frederick: Board of Education of Frederick County, 1975.

———. *Frederick County, Maryland: Never the Like Again*. Frederick: the Heritage Partnership, 1995.

Harwood, Herbert H. Jr. *Impossible Challenge II: Baltimore to Washington and Harper's Ferry from 1828 to 1994*. Baltimore, MD: Barnard, Roberts and Co., 1994.

Haugh, Christopher E. *Monocacy: The Pre-History of Frederick County, Maryland*. Videorecording. Frederick: Chris Haugh/GS Communications, 1999.

———. *Up from the Meadows: A History of Black Americans in Frederick County, Maryland*. Videorecording. Frederick: Frederick Cablevision, 1997.

Heerbrandt, Katherine. "HOPE VI: Cure for housing ills?" *Frederick News-Post*. 30 July 2003: Sec. A-1.

Helfenstein, Ernest. *History of All Saints' Parish, Frederick County, Maryland*. 2nd ed. Frederick: All Saints Church, 1991.

Historical Society of Frederick County. Frederick: vertical files.

"The History of the Weinberg." www.weinbergcenter.org/general/history.cfm.

Hitselberger, Mary Fitzhugh and John Philip Dern. *Bridge in Time: The Complete 1850 Census of Frederick County, Maryland*. Redwood City, CA: Monocacy Book Company, 1978.

Jones, Michael D. "Asks commissioner to oppose Blue Law vote." *Frederick News-Post*. 8 December 1980: Sec. A-6.

Lebherz, Richard. *The Long and Intriguing Journey of the C. Burr Artz Library*. Frederick: Corporate Color, Inc., 2002.

———. *Windows on Frederick: A Glimpse into Frederick's Historic Past*. Frederick: Diversions Publications, 2001.

Malik, M.A. "4 appeals may affect Frederick." *Frederick News-Post*. 30 November 1979: Sec. A-1.

Moyer, Teresa S. and Dean Herrin. "The Journey Ahead: Meriwether Lewis in Harpers Ferry and Frederick." *Catoctin History* 2.1 (2003): 30–34.

———. " 'The Most Gigantic Men We Have Ever Seen:' Indian Delegations in the Catoctin Region." *Catoctin History* 2.1 (2003): 36–37.

Fort Detrick Maryland, A Community of Excellence. San Diego, CA: MARCOA Publishing Inc., 1995.

Onley, Joy Hall. *Dear Old Faithful Lincoln*. Frederick: Corporate Color Publishing Co., 1999.

———, ed. *Memories of Frederick . . . Over on the Other Side: Highlights of the History of Blacks in Frederick County: the Way it Was . . . Including the Memories of 19 Blacks Who Have Spent the Majority of Their Years Living Here*. Frederick: Joy Hall Onley, 1995.

Randall, Frances A. *Mirror on Frederick through 250 Years*. Frederick: Great Southern Printing and Manufacturing Co., 1998.

———. "Frederick life 1880s–1980s, The latest inventions begin to be part of the local scene." *Frederick News-Post*, Hello Frederick supplement. 20 July 2003: 3.

Reimer, Terry. *One Vast Hospital: The Civil War Hospital Sites in Frederick, Maryland after Antietam*. Frederick: National Museum of Civil War Medicine, 2001.

Reed, Amy Lee Huffman and Marie LaForge Burns. *In and Out of Frederick Town: Colonial Occupations*. Frederick: Amy Lee Huffman Reed and Marie LaForge Burns, 1985.

Rice, Millard Milburn. *This Was the Life: Excerpts from the Judgment Records of Frederick County, Maryland 1748–1765*. Baltimore, MD: Genealogical Publishing Co., 1984.

Scharf, J. Thomas. *History of Western Maryland.* Reprint of 1882 edition. Baltimore, MD: Regional Publishing Company, 1968.

Schildknecht, C.E., ed. *Monocacy and Catoctin. Vol. 1: Some Early Settlers of Frederick and Carroll Counties, MD and Adams County, PA and Descendants 1725–1985.* Shippensburg, PA: Beidel Printing House, Inc., 1985.

————. *Monocacy and Catoctin. Vol. 3: Additions and Corrections to The History of Frederick County, Maryland by T.J.C. Williams and Folger McKinsey.* Shippensburg, PA: Beidel Printing House, Inc., 1989.

Slagle, Eric. "Schools adapt, adopt: Face of Frederick education has changed in 50 years." *Frederick News-Post.* 25 May 2003: 1.

Thomas, Ronald, Kenneth Baumgardt, Merle Dunn, and Robert F. Hoffman. *Archeological Data Recovery at the Birely Tannery (18FR575), City of Frederick, Maryland.* Newark, DE: MAAR Associates, 1991.

Tracey, Grace L. and John Philip Dern. *Pioneers of Old Monocacy: the Early Settlement of Frederick County, Maryland 1721–1743.* Baltimore, MD: Genealogical Publishing Co., 1987.

URS Corporation. *Final Environmental Assessment for the Five-Year Capital Improvement Program at Frederick Municipal Airport.* Prepared for the Federal Aviation Administration, Washington Airports District Office. Hunt Valley, MD: URS Corporation, 2002.

Waters, Ed Jr. "Hess's won't open Sunday: Chamber panel backs laws." *Frederick News-Post.* 30 November 1979: Sec. A-1.

————. "Frederick Chamber takes stand on blue laws, with provision." *Frederick News-Post.* 18 April 1980: Sec. B-5.

Wentz, Abdel Ross. *The Lutheran Church of Frederick, Maryland 1738–1938.* Harrisburg, PA: The Evangelical Press, 1938.

"What a difference, but can it last?" *Frederick News-Post.* 15 July 2003: Sec. A-8.

Williams, T.J.C. and Folger McKinsey. *History of Frederick County, Maryland.* Reprint of 1910 edition. Baltimore, MD: Regional Publishing Company, 1979.

Williamson, Elizabeth. "EPA Funding Assists City in Turning Over Old Lots." *The Washington Post.* 10 August 2003: Sec. C-5.

Wolf, Herb III. *Houses of Worship in Frederick, Maryland, A 250-Year History 1745–1995.* Baltimore, MD: Gateway Press, 1995.

Zeigler, Mark. "Remembering the Class D, Blue Ridge League 1915–1918, 1920–30." www.blueridgeleague.org/home.htm

INDEX

Index